ROMAN CATHOLIC EXEGESIS SINCE
DIVINO AFFLANTE SPIRITU

SOCIETY
OF BIBLICAL
LITERATURE

DISSERTATION SERIES
J. J. M. Roberts, Old Testament Editor
Charles Talbert, New Testament Editor

Number 111
ROMAN CATHOLIC EXEGESIS SINCE
DIVINO AFFLANTE SPIRITU
Hermeneutical Implications
by
Robert Bruce Robinson

Robert Bruce Robinson

ROMAN CATHOLIC EXEGESIS SINCE
DIVINO AFFLANTE SPIRITU

Hermeneutical Implications

Scholars Press
Atlanta, Georgia

ROMAN CATHOLIC EXEGESIS SINCE *DIVINO AFFLANTE SPIRITU*
Hermeneutical Implications

Robert Bruce Robinson

Library of Congress Cataloging-in-Publication Data

Robinson, Robert Bruce.
    Roman Catholic exegesis since Divino afflante
spiritu.

    (Dissertation series / Society of Biblical
Literature ; no. 11)
    Thesis (Ph.D.)--Yale University, 1982.
    Bibliography: p.
    I. Bible--Criticism, interpretation, etc.--
History--20th century. 2. Catholic Church--Doctrines--
History--20th century. 3. Brown, Raymond Edward--
Contributions in Biblical criticism. 4. Alonso Schokel,
Luis, 1920-   --Contributions in Biblical criticism.
5. Lohfink, Norbert--Contributions in Biblical criticism.
6. Bible--Hermeneutics. I. Title. II. Series:
Dissertation series (Society of Biblical Literature) ;
no. 11.
BS500.R6   1988   200.6'01   88-11432
ISBN 1-55540-240-2 (alk. paper)
ISBN 1-55540-241-0 (pbk.)

Printed in the United States of America
on acid-free paper

Preface

I am happy to acknowledge a great debt to my advisor, Brevard S. Childs, for his advice and encouragement, both directly and through his example. Thanks are also due Hans Frei, who stimulated the original paper from which this study grew and on several occasions helped focus the issues involved in it. My thanks also go to my friends and fellow students Harry Nasuti and Tim Polk for their willingness to listen and share their insight.

I would like to thank Ms. Susan Chiasson for her accurate and efficient typing of the manuscript and my wife, Joanna, ultimately for support that goes beyond thanking, but here for her painstaking editing.

All citations from the Bible except those within quotations from other works are from the Revised Standard Version. The abbreviations of the titles of journals, periodicals, and serials are according to the *Member's Handbook* of The Society of Biblical Literature, eds. George MacRae and Paul J. Achtemeier (Chico, CA: Scholar's Press, 1980), pp. 90-97.

Table of Contents

Preface...v

Chapter 1
Introduction: The Catholic Hermeneutical Discussion Up to
Divino Afflante Spiritu...1

Chapter 2
Sensus Plenior..29

Chapter 3
Luis Alonso-Schökel 57

Chapter 4
Norbert Lohfink 105

Chapter 5
Conclusion: Toward a Consistent Literary Model...................149

Bibliography..179

Chapter 1

Introduction: The Catholic Hermeneutical Discussion Up to *Divino Afflante Spiritu*

With justice, the history of critical Catholic biblical scholarship is divided into two distinct epochs: the period before the promulgation of *Divino Afflante Spiritu* and the period after. The great encyclical, issued by Pope Pius XII on September 30, 1943, has rightly been called the Magna Charta of Catholic critical scholarship.[1] Catholic scholars had undertaken critical studies before the encyclical, but the Church's official posture toward their work had been uncertain at best. Frequently critical works met with a suspicious or openly hostile reception. The fifty years since the encyclical *Providentissimus Deus*, whose anniversary Pius XII commemorated with his own pronouncement, had witnessed the acrimony of the Modernist crisis with its legacy of bitterness and suspicion. In its aftermath, critical scholars labored under the shadow of official disapproval, burdened by the sense that Church authorities hovered at their shoulders, scrutinizing their work for traces of Modernist impurity. The uncertainty of Rome's attitude, which was often difficult to gauge, inhibited creative scholarship. *Divino Afflante Spiritu* cut through the uncertainty and suspicion and at a stroke completely reversed the Church's official position. The encyclical expressed confidence both in Catholic biblical critics and in the methods they employed to interpret the biblical texts. Certain of these methods, most notably form criticism, were not only sanctioned for the first time, but made virtually mandatory by the pontiff.

The effects of the encyclical were prompt and dramatic. Catholic critical scholarship, which languished in the heavy Modernist and post-Modernist atmosphere of official suspicion and disapproval, drew a

---

1 Thomas A. Collins and Raymond E. Brown, "Church Pronouncements," *The Jerome Biblical Commentary*, eds. Raymond E. Brown, Joseph P. Fitzmyer, and Roland O. Murphy (Englewood Cliffs: Prentice-Hall, 1968), p. 625.

draft of fresh life from *Divino Afflante Spiritu*. Catholic critical studies flourished. In the post-war period a new generation of Catholic exegetes joined the ranks of the most distinguished biblical scholars. In many areas Catholic scholars, responding to the encouragement of the encyclical, are currently in the forefront of critical research.

There is much to celebrate in the revitalization of Catholic scholarly engagement with the Bible which the official acceptance of criticism has fostered. At the same time the rise to predominance of critical methodology has produced a new range of problems, particularly concerning the traditional theological understanding and use of the Bible. Jean Gribomont indicates the nature of the new tension.

> Much lost time has been made up. For Catholics the encyclical *Divino Afflante Spiritu* authorized the first step. But by their very breadth the results achieved pose a second series of problems: how may one effect a synthesis between the strictly historical sense and traditional Christian exegesis, not stopping at the words of a man to his contemporaries, but finding the word of God, living and efficacious, *ad nostram doctrinam scripta*.[2]

Gribomont points to two related problems. First is the difficulty in effecting a synthesis between the results of the new critical methods and traditional exegesis. Precritical exegesis moves on such divergent lines from its modern critical successor that the two do not seem to converge at any apparent point. The divergence may seem to be just in the nature of the case and hardly to be expected otherwise, but the seriousness of the matter becomes apparent when we realize that both the precritical and the modern critical methods claimed to define the same thing, the true sense of the scriptural texts. More pointedly, critical scholarship claims to supersede the precritical description of the sense of the text. Problems spring up precisely because the precritical understanding of the text discredited or superseded by critical interpretations underlies the fundamental theology traditionally held by the Church. The great founders of the Church together with its most influential theologians based their theological reflection on interpretations of the Scriptures, both Old and New Testaments, which modern scholars would consider invalid. One need only think of the many New Testament sayings which have traditionally been interpreted as words of Jesus but which modern scholarship ascribes to the early Church to

---

2 Jean Gribomont, "Sens plénier, sens typique et sens littéral," in *Problémes et méthode d'exégèse théologiques*, ed. L. Cerfaux (Bruges and Paris: De Brouwer, 1950), p. 21. All translations in which the title is given in the original language are my own.

see the problem in all its force. Is all precritical theology to be discarded because it is based on a misunderstanding of the nature of these texts? The effect, then, of modern critical scholarship is to cut scriptural support from under traditional theology, leaving it to search for other bases for its authority. At the same time a wedge is driven between Scripture, now perceived to have a sense unrecognized for millennia, and traditional interpretation, which is quite distinct and unrelated to the true sense so recently discovered. The Church is cut off from its roots.

The tension between tradition and Scripture may seem a uniquely Catholic problem. Without doubt the problem takes a particularly intense form within the Catholic Church because tradition is formally recognized as authoritative alongside Scripture, so that when the two appear in conflict, the difficulty is acute. But the principle of *sola scriptura* does not preclude Protestant denominations from preserving informal yet nonetheless deeply entrenched traditions both about how Scripture is to be understood and about what Scripture teaches. The problem is perhaps most apparent in conservative denominations in which a tradition of literal reading of the Bible confronts the fact that the congregation is composed of twentieth-century believers. But the gap is equally obvious in more liberal churches in which the Bible is used liturgically in ways long since undercut by critical scholarship. The problem is general.

The second problem is broader, involving the applicability of the results of critical scholarship to the shaping of contemporary theology and the practice of the Church. Without question modern critical methodologies have introduced great precision and sophistication to the production of information about the biblical books, their preliterary background, the historical period in which they were written, the identity and circumstances of their authors, and so on through the critical programs. But there has not been a comparable advance in the application of that information to the theology or practice of the Church. This constitutes a grave problem because the Church's interest in the Bible is in its character as *"ad nostram doctrinam scripta."* Methodologies, programs of research, hermeneutical considerations are, in effect, all instrumental and are measured, in practice, by their effectiveness in making the Bible's own instruction lucid and comprehensible. Since *Divino Afflante Spiritu,* Catholic scholars have joined other biblical investigators in prodigies of scholarly research but without commensurate success in directing the results of that research to the essential task of the Church of shaping faith and practice. This phenomenon is likewise not unknown in Protestant churches.

It should not be supposed that Gribomont was the only Catholic scholar sensitive to the problems emerging after *Divino Afflante Spiritu*. Nearly all Catholic scholars were concerned about the problems and addressed them in different ways. The diversity of responses makes generalizing hazardous, but a few observations may be risked. With regard to the first problem, the relationship of critical research to traditional belief, the attitude has been a carefully tempered "let the chips fall where they may." The hard-won acceptance of critical methodologies carried with it the right to define the sense of the text and the crucial right to the free employment of the methodologies. If the traditional understanding of the text did not agree with the critical understanding, either the traditional understanding had to give ground to the modern interpretation or the question was adjourned until further information eased the tension. Critical scholars showed no inclination to modify critical conclusions exclusively because they did not agree with tradition. Associated with this attitude was often a barely concealed suspicion of scholars who held too closely to traditional exegesis, a fear of backsliding and reaction that would undo the advances initiated by the encyclical. This general attitude was tempered in several ways. Catholic scholars have tended to be very careful and conservative in their consideration of texts on which much depends in traditional theology; they are particularly circumspect in their approach to New Testament texts. Tradition has a gravity to which the critics are sensitive. Further, there is a tendency to interpret passages in a manner consistent with traditional beliefs wherever this is possible without compromising critical principles. A good example is New Testament passages apparently referring to Jesus' brothers, which many Catholic exegetes interpret to refer to cousins, an interpretation defensible on the Greek usage of the time, in order to preserve the perpetual virginity of Mary, a traditional belief. Finally, there have been efforts to define some other way in which traditional interpretations are related to the biblical texts than as their literal sense. Many critical scholars adhered to the theory of a *sensus plenior*, which will be considered in detail later, as a way to maintain the relation of traditional interpretations to the text without denying the preeminence of critical study. None of these approaches resolves fully the tension between criticism and traditional exegesis, although they do establish a tenuous *modus vivendi*.

Introduction

The second problem, that of general practical and theological application, has likewise occasioned several types of response. Critical research, through disciplines such as philology and archeology, provides new information which directly illuminates obscure practices and words and casts light on poorly understood details. The contribution in this area is neither to be disputed nor undervalued. But random commentary on obscure details is not a full program and has only superficial impact on the larger task of theology. In fact, in the period just after *Divino Afflante Spiritu* Catholic scholars did not develop a uniquely Catholic theological program based on the newly open critical methodologies. Rather, they joined in the existing Protestant programs, with necessary adjustments made for the differences in tradition. Critical scholarship, at least theoretically, was "presuppositionless," so Catholics could enter the critical theological debate on equal footing with Protestant scholars, even if they entered from a slightly different angle and assumed a slightly different perspective. In this country pioneering Catholic critical scholars such as Bruce Vawter and John L. McKenzie resided easily within the loose bounds of the Biblical Theology Movement, despite some differences. The Biblical Theology Movement's program had several parts. Critical study revealed within the Bible Israel's own record of "God who acts," in G. Ernest Wright's memorable phrase; history is transformed to salvation history, its sacral dimension emphasized. Critical study further revealed distinctive Hebrew and Greek mentalities. To think biblically was to think using these mentalities. Both parts of this program assumed that critical study could itself develop theologically significant categories, either of history or national psychology.

The Biblical Theology Movement has largely disintegrated and it is questionable how deeply critically secured historical principles penetrated into the practice of theology, either formally or informally in the actual usage of the Church.[3] Martin Noth, a giant among biblical historians, at the height of the interest in historical categories lamented that students departing the German universities to parishes promptly committed a *sacrificium intellectus*, leaving most of their impressive historical training behind.[4] Noth's own suggestion that the ancient historical events be made present (*vergegenwärtigt*) through

3 See Brevard S. Childs, *Biblical Theology in Crisis* (Philadelphia: Westminster Press, 1970), pp. 51-96.
4 Martin Noth, "Die Vergegenwärtigung des Alten Testaments in der Verkündigung," *EvT* 12 (1952/53), p. 9.

preaching provided no direct indications how transference of past acts to the present would be possible.

There have been other efforts, of course, to develop theological categories from within critical study itself and Catholics have participated in the discussion. But no approach has managed to garner anything like a consensus and the fragmentation has been so general that the possibility of the theological use of critical results has emerged as a disputable point. Scholars have not been able to turn around from their deep and controlled penetration into the background of the text to announce equally deep and controlled theological insights. The element of control is important. Compared to the rigorous, carefully controlled research on the historical context of the text, the reverse movement theologically from the text has appeared embarrassingly subjective. Many scholars as a consequence have demurred from indicating any theological application, offering their work as a contribution to the better understanding of the biblical world pending any breakthroughs in theological use of such information. Biblical study has been broken into two phases, critical study and theological application. The first flourishes, the second languishes in neglect.

The relatively modest theological contribution of critical scholarship and the inability to resolve the tension between modern criticism and tradition on strictly critical grounds has been alarming to the Church, whose interest in the Bible is as "*ad nostram doctrinam scripta*." The two problems are of a fundamentally hermeneutical character. The hermeneutical principles developed within the boundaries of historical criticism have proven too narrow to resolve the problems. A few Catholic scholars have therefore begun to venture outside the *arrondissement* of historical critical hermeneutics to explore other hermeneutical avenues. Several of those explorations will be considered in the following chapters. It is essential to be very clear that the scholars studied do not reject critical scholarship. There were, and are, reactionaries who yearn for the precritical exegesis of the days before *Divino Afflante Spiritu*, but the scholars to be considered here are not to be confounded with them. All presuppose and explicitly acknowledge the validity of critical scholarship. Yet, without denigrating critical scholarship, all would agree that a hermeneutical task remains after *Divino Afflante Spiritu*. Critical scholarship must be brought within the ongoing tradition of the Church and made productive for faith and practice.

Divino Afflante Spiritu officially opened the door to critical scholarship for Catholic exegetes by sanctioning particular resolutions of hermeneutical and theological problems which had blocked the way previously. The character of the resolutions the encyclical sanctioned established the direction of modern Catholic exegesis, including the somewhat divergent exegetical approaches to be studied here. All Catholic exegetes moved forward from this fixed point, if at somewhat different angles. But for its part, the encyclical was shaped by the nature of the issues it sought to resolve. Those issues roiled to the surface in the cauldron known as the Modernist crisis and the resolutions appeared clearly only once that cauldron ceased to boil. For all the influence *Divino Afflante Spiritu* has had on the development of recent exegesis, it looks backward to the Modernist crisis for the issues it addresses.

The theological use of Scripture at the onset of the Modernist period was static, excessively narrow, and turned in upon itself. Neo-scholasticism dominated the theological discussion and the theological manuals of the day were pale reflections of the *Summa* of Thomas Aquinas. So great was the regard for Aquinas that Scripture was no longer used with vigor and originality to address the immediate theological concerns of the day, as it had been in his hands, but in a derivative fashion, to explicate the teaching of the master himself.[5] Scripture was subordinated to dogmatics. The biblical text construed quite literally — a realistic narrative reading was the common mode of reading among the clergy — provided inspired and therefore divinely guaranteed immutable premises. Thomistic principles governed, chief among them that theological argument should be based on the literal sense of the text.[6] By literal sense Aquinas had meant the plain sense of the words themselves, as distinguished from spiritual senses, which derived from the sense of the things to which the words referred. Aquinas' understanding of the literal sense was precritical in the sense made clear by Hans Frei in *The Eclipse of Biblical Narrative*.[7] That the literal sense referred to actual historical events was an assumption im-

---

5   See Luis Alonso-Schökel's assessment of the theological manuals in "Argument d'Ecriture et théologie biblique dans l'enseignement théologique," *NRT* 4 (1959), pp. 337-354.

6   "Thus in Holy Scripture no confusion results, for all the senses are founded on one — the literal — from which alone can any argument be drawn" (Thomas Aquinas, *Summa Theologica*, I, q. 1, a. 10).

7   Hans Frei, *The Eclipse of Biblical Narrative* (New Haven and London: Yale University Press, 1974), pp. 1-50.

plied by the meaningfulness of the text, not a hypothesis to be demonstrated. Aquinas' theological arguments were premised on a precritical literal reading of Scripture, though it must be stressed that individual arguments were not necessarily predicated on a connected, narrative reading, that is, a reading of a verse in its full literary context. Individual verses, read literally, contained divine truth upon which theological reflection could build. There was little need in this theological use for a specifically biblical science, since the text was perfectly plain in its literal sense.

In the intervening years between Aquinas and the Modernist period, changes occurred in what was meant by the literal meaning of a text, particularly in the area of referentiality. For Aquinas the reference of Scripture to events in the history of Israel or the life of Jesus or the Church had been assumed; meaningful language was referential and Scripture was meaningful. No historical demonstration was necessary because referentiality was included in a linguistic rule. But, as Frei shows, in the eighteenth century new historical interest and achievements in historical research opened a fissure between the account in the text and the actual events to which the text referred. The actual events could be established independently of the text by the examination of evidence and the application of reason.[8] What for Aquinas had been an implication of the meaningfulness of a text, by the nineteenth century even in Catholic circles was transformed into a historical hypothesis, though of a peculiar type. Because of the weight of theological doctrine riding on the hypothesis that the biblical texts referred accurately to actual events, Catholic scholars could not admit that it was a hypothesis subject to the logic of verification or disconfirmation applicable to all other historical hypotheses, but treated it as a dogmatic fact, subject to no further inquiry. The defense of Scripture took on a very hard edge as the question of truth leapt to the center of the discussion.

The vulnerability of the theological use of Scripture implied by this situation was extraordinary. After the encyclical *Providentissimus* of 1893 reaffirmed the inerrancy of Scripture, a position it could hardly have avoided, an anonymous article in the *Contemporary Review* stated the situation succinctly.

> Since the publication of the papal encyclical, the Bible has become a kind of Prince Rupert's drop; one has only to break the tiniest bit from the end of it,

---

8   Ibid., pp. 51-65.

and it breaks into a thousand pieces. For today's Catholic, the Bible, the
Catholic Church, Christianity and Revelation, everything—depends on the
accuracy of the Scriptural count of Esau's wives.[9]

The eighteenth century had replaced the sure foundation of Scripture
supporting dogmatic teaching with an ever more dubious historical
proposition.

The extreme narrowness of the problem and yet its supreme importance need to be noted, if only to understand the passions of the Modernist crisis. Neo-scholastic propositional use of Scripture, the use most
at jeopardy, was the most prominent Catholic mode of employing
Scripture, the closest to the center of Catholic doctrine. Aquinas and
the *Summa* enjoyed a unique authority recognized at the First Vatican
Council and neo-scholasticism especially flourished under the
patronage of Pope Leo XIII, whose long papacy encompassed most of
the period of the rise of Modernist thought. Although a nascent biblical criticism emerged in this period, it did not become self-reflective
enough to form truly biblical theology. Nor was there a deeply rooted
tradition of literal reading of the Bible among the laity that might have
given rise to broader theological reflection. Theological use of Scripture simply was neo-scholastic. If the scriptural base of that particular
use was challenged, as it was increasingly by historical criticism, the
whole fabric of Catholic theology as it then existed threatened to un-
ravel.

The challenge was severe. Although the neo-scholastic use of Scripture was very narrow, it was not insulated. Catholic scholars in
countries such as England and Germany where Protestants
predominated were in constant contact with Protestant scholars. At
Tübingen the university had a newly established Catholic faculty
alongside the more famous Protestant faculty under F. C. Baur. The
works of Protestant higher critics were certainly read, as witness the
polemics undertaken against them. Increasingly, despite rearguard actions, it proved impossible to eradicate the influence of critical biblical scholarship or to combat the influence of philosophers such as
Kant, Hegel, Schleiermacher, and the empiricist philosophers of
science, all of whom undermined the Thomistic system. The Catholic
laity, although largely sealed out of any direct role in the development
of formal theology, was not immune to the general critical, scientific

9 "The Encyclical and English and American Catholics," *Contemporary
Review*, April 1894, quoted in F.-M. Braun, *The Work of Père Lagrange,*
trans. Richard T. A. Murphy (Milwaukee: Bruce Publishing Co., 1963), p. 77.

spirit of the age. In fact, partly because they were sealed out of the formal theological debate, many members of the emerging educated middle class in Europe were sympathetic to the critical approach to the
Scripture. Renan's *Life of Jesus* caused a sensation in France when it
was published in 1863. A gulf opened between the intellectual assumptions then current everywhere and those underlying the neo-scholastic
use of Scripture.

Catholic scholars were also not shielded from the rush of discoveries
made particularly in the areas of philology and archeology which expanded knowledge of the ancient world exponentially and provided
ever new grist for the critics' mill. The continual advancement of the
sciences, including what the age considered the historical sciences,
threw Catholic apologists onto the defensive. Each new imputation of
inaccuracy required a response. These responses were increasingly
forced and unconvincing, the apologists compelled continually to dig
deeper into their ingenuity. Alfred Loisy, later the central figure in the
Modernist controversies over the Bible, recalled the apologetic lectures he attended as a student under Abbé Vigouroux, then Professor
of Bible at the Catholic Institute in Paris and perhaps the most
respected orthodox biblical scholar in France at the time. Loisy
recalled,

> One found it easy, for instance, to abandon all belief in the flood of Genesis
> after hearing the professor explain gravely that the passages attributed to the
> Yahwist writer (after the source in which God is given the name Yahwe) are
> a description of what was going on in the Eternal mind, while the passages
> called Elohist (after the source which employs as the divine name the collec-
> tive noun Elohim) have regard to the revelation of these thoughts to Noah,
> and their practical execution; that, the flood covering only the then inhabited
> portions of the earth, the ark was plenty large enough to contain all the animal
> species known to Noah; that a calculation had been made, and the ark shown
> to be capable of enclosing six thousand, six hundred and sixty-six species, al-
> lowing so much cubic space to each couple — and much more of this same
> sort! I could not endure this childishness. To swallow it, one must have made
> up his mind beforehand to accept any reasons, however puerile, to buttress
> a foregone conclusion.[10]

It was clear to many well before matters reached the state of
Vigouroux's lectures in the 1870's and '80's that this sort of continous
ad hoc defense against critical challenge had to be replaced by more
general considerations or the whole dogmatic theological edifice

---

10 Alfred Loisy, *My Duel with the Vatican*, trans. Richard W. Boynton
(New York: E. P. Dutton, Inc., 1924), p. 89.

would collapse under the weight of the buttresses built to defend it. Apologetic was strained to the point of fracture by the requirement of defending every detail of the biblical accounts, lest error be admitted and the foundations of dogmatic propositions reduced to sand. In order to preserve the essential, it was necessary to distinguish between what could and must be defended and what could not and need not. One major approach emerged early.

August Rohling, a professor of Old Testament at Münster, proposed a very obvious distinction in the journal *Natur und Offenbarung* in 1872.[11] Viewed theologically there were three types of material in the Bible: first, matters of faith and morals; second, historical facts on which matters of faith and morals depended; third, completely profane matters. Rohling argued that inspiration, which conferred inerrancy, was restricted to the first two categories. In regard to profane matters, the human author was left to his own devices and, like all humans, could err. This approach is typical of the period. It accepts the critical position that there are errors in the Bible and thereby relieves the direct pressure on scholars called upon to defend the last detail. But it also renders the admission of error theologically inconsequential, because errors do not occur in matters pertaining to faith and morals. The inerrant premises of dogmatic theology remain under the guarantee of inspiration.

With some variation in detail, Rohling's distinction was the working assumption of Catholic scholars drawn toward criticism. It is essentially similar to Cardinal Newman's better known exclusion of *obiter dicta* from inspiration. Lenormant, a French Catholic lay historian, endorsed a similar view but further distinguished between revelation and inspiration. In Italy di Bartolo took a slightly different tack but arrived at nearly the same point by maintaining the traditional position that the whole Bible was inspired, but distinguishing, no doubt coincidentally, three levels of inspiration. The lowest level did not confer inerrancy.[12]

On the essential point, that where the Bible referred to matters affecting faith and morals, it was fully inspired and its propositions therefore incontrovertible verities, there was no break with Catholic orthodoxy in this proposal. Nonetheless, the Catholic Church was not prepared to admit a distinction in inspiration that would fragment Scripture according to critical principles outside its control and also

---

11 See Anthony C. Cotter, "The Antecedents of the Encyclical *Providentissimus Deus*," *CBQ* 5 (1943), p. 118.
12 Ibid., pp. 119-122.

reduce the authority and dignity of Scripture. The principle of a unitary and uniform inspiration of Scripture was derived from the fact that God was the principal author of Scripture and therefore responsible for the content of the Bible. The human author was simply the instrument through which God communicated. To impute error to the Bible in any respect was to impute error to God. This principle, which focused the issue of inerrancy on God's authorship, was given classic formulation at the First Vatican Council in 1870. In a famous passage the Constitution *Dei Filius* proclaimed:

> These books of the Old and New Testament are to be received as sacred and canonical in their integrity with all their parts, as they are enumerated in the decree of the said Council [Trent] and are contained in the ancient Latin edition of the Vulgate. These the Church holds to be sacred and canonical, not because, having been carefully composed by mere human industry, they were later approved by her authority, not merely because they contain revelation with no admixture of error, but because, having been written by the inspiration of the Holy Spirit, they have God for their author and have been delivered as such to the Church herself.[13]

Pope Leo XIII reaffirmed this principle in the encyclical *Providentissimus Deus* of 1893 and cited it explicitly to exclude the suggestion that errors could be attributed to the human authors.[14] The authority of the Bible rested on God's direct authorship of it, which allowed no division. And the principle of God's authorship likewise admitted of no suggestion of error.

Scholars who suggested a limitation on inspiration as the basis of a possible accommodation with critical scholarship were essentially mediators; they did not propose a new model of theological use of Scripture but sought to integrate new information into the orthodox use of Scripture. *Providentissimus Deus* cut them off. Of a far different stripe was Alfred Loisy, the center of the fire storm that broke out over Modernist interpretation of the Bible. Loisy too subscribed to critical methods, because the times and the state of knowledge demanded

---

13 First Vatican Council, Chapter Two, "On Revelation," *Constitution Dei Filius,* in *Official Catholic Teachings: Bible Interpretation,* ed. James J. Megivern (Wilmington, NC: McGrath Publishing Co., 1978), p. 191; also cf. *Enchiridion Symbolorum Definitionum et Declarationum de Rebus Fidei et Morum,* eds. Henry Denzinger and Adolf Schonmetzer, 33rd edition (Barcelona: Herder, 1965), 3006. Hereafter, all references to the *Enchiridion* will be indicated by D & S followed by the appropriate reference number.

14 Pope Leo XIII, *Providentissimus Deus* in Megivern, *Bible Interpretation,* p. 216; also cf. D & S 3286.

them. But Loisy was not in the least interested in the apologetic task of locating a *modus vivendi* between criticism and orthodoxy which would have the least possible impact on neo-scholastic dogmatics. Neo-scholasticism needed to be superseded by a new theology resting on the sound footing of critically secured principles. Loisy later recalled that in his school days he had studied the *Summa* of Aquinas and had learned systematic thought from it. But the arguments themselves had not moved him.[15] What the times required was a reformulation of doctrine, a restructuring of the whole system in the light of modern knowledge, a reformulation comparable in scope to what Aquinas had done in the thirteenth century on the basis of Aristotelian philosophy.

Loisy further saw that the apologetic attempts to separate the profane chaff from the sacred wheat left few precious grains on the threshing floor. In Adolf von Harnack's *Das Wesen des Christentums*, a book of immense influence among liberal Protestants, Loisy thought he saw the logical conclusion of a critical program that peeled back the later additions to arrive at the original kernel, the essence of Christian faith, "faith in God the Father, as revealed by Jesus Christ."[16]

In *The Gospel and the Church*, Loisy's response to Harnack and perhaps his most controversial book, Loisy opposed the severe reductionism involved in casting away everything historically conditioned or attributable to the faith of the early church in order to isolate a timeless essence, an assured universal, even if it was only a single abstract principle. Loisy considered the reductionism a reflection of the attenuated faith of liberal Protestantism. But submerged beneath Harnack's work was also a false interpretive principle in the assumption that there was a timeless, unchanging essence independent of the historical development of Christian doctrine and the Church. This notion was radically false, false on the very historical principles on which Harnack conducted his work. There was no immutable essence out-

---

15 Loisy, *My Duel*, p. 78.
16 Alfred Loisy, *The Gospel and the Church*, trans. Christopher Home, Lives of Jesus Series (Philadelphia: Fortress Press, 1976), p. 3.

side the historical process, nor could there be, since it is the law of everything historical to change. Loisy's counterproposal to Harnack's critical reductionism was to acknowledge that the whole of Christian tradition, including the work and teaching of Christ, was subject to that same law of historical change and evolution. This acknowledgment did not imply any denigration of the value of the tradition, since it was the essential nature of history to change and develop.[17] Historical development represented a debasement of originally pure principles (Harnack's position) only if one assumed there were unchanging principles passed down by history but unaffected by it. Loisy regarded this idea as patently absurd and conclusively disproven by a study of history.[18]

In place of immutable principles, Loisy saw the course of historical development itself. History moved forward and both Christian doctrine and the Church developed and changed. But what assurance was there that the change was according to the will of God if there were no immutable principles that change followed? Loisy responded by appealing to the historical continuity which existed between Jesus' work and teaching and the Church. There was no radical gap between the work of Jesus and the emergence of the Church, as if the Church were a perversion of Jesus' work or Church doctrine a falsification of Christ's pristine teaching. Jesus' work continued in the Church and the historical change and development which was the nature of everything historical took place within the body of the Church. Authority therefore resided with the Church, although it was not the authority of the possessor of immutable truth but the authority of the body within which legitimate historical growth took place.

---

17 "Jesus foretold the kingdom, and it was the Church that came; she came, enlarging the form of the gospel, which it was impossible to preserve as it was, as soon as the Passion closed the ministry of Jesus. There is no institution on the earth or in history whose status and value may not be questioned if the principle is established that nothing may exist except in its original form. Such a principle is contrary to the law of life, which is movement and a continual effort of adaptation to conditions always new and perpetually changing." (Ibid., p. 166).

18 Ibid., p. 217.

The response to *The Gospel and the Church* was hardly what Loisy could have expected for a defense of the Church against liberal Protestantism. Cardinal Richard, the Archbishop of Paris, went directly to Rome and had the book condemned. This was perhaps predictable. Richard was strictly orthodox. But M.-J. Lagrange, who had been sympathetic to Loisy's critical work, though sometimes alarmed by it, broke with Loisy and moved to dissociate himself from Loisy's brand of criticism.[19]

Loisy's historical criticism led to conclusions as radical as Harnack's. In effect Loisy had followed the historical referentiality and historical conditionality of the text outside the Bible to the actual events themselves and then, not surprisingly, found the significance of those events in the historical process of which they were a part. The approach is certainly consistent, but it implies the practical irrelevance of the biblical texts, because the process of historical development progresses beyond the stage represented by the biblical text. There is, it is true, an organic relationship between the present stage of the development in the Church and its origins, but authority resides in the present moment. The past is relegated to insignificance. The Church clearly could not adopt a program that implied the irrelevance of its Scriptures. *The Gospel and the Church* was condemned and Loisy eventually excommunicated. As Loisy showed in *Simples réflexions*, the major anti-Modernist decree of the Holy Office, *Lamentabili Sane Exitu* (1907), referred in most of its specific condemnations to his writings. For example, the decree condemns the propositions:

54. Dogmas, sacraments, hierarchy, both as regards the notion of them and the reality, are but interpretations and evolutions of the Christian intelligence which by external increments have increased and perfected the little germ latent in the gospel.

58. Truth is not any more immutable than man himself, since it is evolved with him, in him, and through him.

---

19 "This time the mask had been cast aside. Loisy not only no longer believed, he was cutting himself off from the Church. The attack he was launching against the Church was the more dangerous because it was presented in her defense. I had, therefore, understood his previous moves badly." (M.-J. Lagrange, *M. Loisy et le modernisme* [Juvisy: Editions du Cerf, 1932], p. 122).

59. Christ did not teach a determinate body of doctrine applicable to all times
and to all men, but rather inaugurated a religious movement adapted or to
be adapted for different times and places.[20]

This decree, the encyclical *Pascendi* of the same year, a series of anticritical decrees of the Pontifical Biblical Commission, and, most
dramatically, Loisy's excommunication brought the Modernist crisis to
a peremptory end. It is important to be clear what was excluded from
the Church. Critical scholarship was not extinguished, though it passed
under a cloud. What was excluded, definitively one must think, was any
principle that denied the relevance of the scriptural text or, more pointedly, the direct relevance of the text for current theology. Loisy had
followed the course laid out by eighteenth-century critics in identifying the meaning of the text with the events to which it referred. That
course led outside the scriptural texts to historical events and processes that followed the laws of history. The text itself became nothing
more than a witness to historical events, and not even a particularly
reliable witness. Scripture was denied its special character as revelation and could not serve as a basis for dogmatic theology. Obviously
neo-scholastic theology was denied outright since it relied on "facts"
that could not be demonstrated historically. The text of Scripture lost
its traditional normative role, displaced by the events and circumstances to which it referred which were integrated into an immanent theology of history. The Church rejected this denigration of Scripture
completely.

The Church also rejected the one-sided balance Loisy had struck
between the two traditional centers of Catholic authority, Scripture
and tradition. Because Scripture, as Loisy (and his opponents) conceived it, was static and the very essence of history was change, Loisy
transferred nearly all authority to tradition, the more dynamic center
of authority, embodied in the Church. Static, however, meant two different things to Loisy and the Church, and both ascribed an entirely
different value to the agreed fact that the text was static. For the
Church, static was equivalent to stable and ultimately reliable. Scripture referred to revealed universal truths. It would constitute a failing
if they were subject to change. In the neo-scholastic worldview, truth
did not change; if it did, it was not truth. Loisy argued on a completely different level. The text was static not because its reference was to

---

20 Congregation of the Inquisition, *Lamentabili* in Megivern, *Bible
Interpretation*, p. 263; also cf. D & S 2054, 2058, 2059.

unchanging truth, but because its reference was to events fixed in a segment of the historical continuum long since passed by. When viewed from the end of the continuum, the present historical moment, that ancient segment appeared static, which implied remote, inaccessible, superseded, irrelevant. Loisy therefore transferred authority to the active participant in historical evolution, the Church. The issue, then, was not whether the text was static — both sides agreed on this — but whether that was good or bad, a blessing or a problem. By excluding Loisy the Church maintained its traditional position that the static nature of Scripture was a blessing, that faith required a solid basis in unchanging truth. This position continued the tension between Scripture and tradition, the static and dynamic principles, without rebalancing the relationship. In particular, there was no adjustment in the balance to take into account the substance of Loisy's insight. As the meaning of Scripture increasingly became identified with its historical reference, it lost its universality to the historical particularity of the events referred to. Banning Loisy was not a resolution of this underlying problem. In the end the effect of so firmly maintaining the traditional balance between Scripture and tradition was to reinforce the view of Scripture as essentially static in content, that it possessed a fixed and unchanging meaning, directly relevant for theology. This principle could only enter into a very complicated and conflicted relationship with the principle of irrelevancy implied by historical criticism which Loisy brought to the fore. The end of the Modernist controversy left intact the view that the meaning of Scripture was static but did not resolve the question whether that fact was to be understood in Loisy's sense or the traditional sense of the Church. Both conceptions remained at work, an important factor in the hermeneutical debate.

In fact, the striking thing about the Modernist crisis is just how many issues went unresolved despite the intensity of the debate. No positive role commensurate with its achievements was defined for criticism. Historical criticism was not brought within the Church; the relationship remained undefined. Loisy had insisted on a completely autonomous and unfettered criticism to which the Church would have to accommodate itself. Theology would have to be brought into line with the critically secured facts. Only criticism that followed its own methodological principles without regard to theological implications was respectable. For its part, the Church, particularly in the decree *Lamentabili*, asserted its absolute authority over all aspects of criticism, even its right to overrule the conclusions of physical science if they conflicted with Church teaching. If anything, the Modernist crisis polarized the positions of both historical critics and the Church, and the decrees and decisions that silenced the Modernists did nothing to resolve the underlying issues.

At the close of the Modernist crisis, then, the Church was still faced with a major problem. The threat Modernism posed to traditional doctrine had been met by suppression of the Modernists, yet no positive role had been given critical scholarship. The Church could not, it was becoming increasingly obvious, forever deny the critical scientific spirit everywhere characteristic of the age. The dilemma comes out somewhat ironically in a letter Loisy wrote to Monsignor Baudrillart, Rector of the Catholic Institute in Paris, after *The Gospel and the Church* and four other of his books had been condemned. Loisy wrote:

> My books of apologetics are in no sense adequate to bring unbelievers and non-Catholics into the fold; they can do no more than dissipate their prejudices against the Catholic idea and, in a certain measure, against the Church. They represent my own endeavor to continue within Catholicism, notwithstanding the impossibility which I found of retaining in their literal sense the bulk of those ideas which constitute Catholic teaching. My writings, therefore, could be of use only to readers in a situation more or less analogous to my own. It may be they have prevented some few desertions; no doubt, as you observe, they have not brought about any conversions.[21]

The new critical methods were not theologically productive, yet there was great danger of losing the faithful who saw their modern scientific worldview in conflict with the Church's precritical formulations. The Church's intellectual respectability was at stake. One must think this was generally recognized. The Catholic professors in German universities were expressly exempted from the anti-Modernist oath that accompanied the decree *Lamentabili* so that they not be humiliated before their Protestant colleagues.[22] For all their appearance of finality, the actions ending the Modernist crisis still left the most important issues open. Actual resolution only came with *Divino Afflante Spiritu* in 1943, a document of a far different, more trusting spirit than

---

21 Quoted in Loisy, *My Duel,* p. 306.
22 See Alec R. Vidler, *The Modernist Movement in the Roman Church: Its Origins and Outcome* (Cambridge: Cambridge University Press, 1934), pp. 202-203.

the anti-Modernist acts. The question is how the Church moved from one position to the other.

The question is not easy to answer. If one looks at official documents, there is little alteration in the anticritical attitude through 1939, when Pius XII acceded to the papacy.[23] Then very abruptly there is a turn toward a far more liberal attitude toward criticism. The obvious explanation is to attribute the change in attitude to the personal influence of the Pope. The Pope's attitude was certainly important. But the Pope's confidence in criticism was predicated on the resolution of the issues described earlier; his sanction on criticism could not have come were criticism and traditional theology still so directly opposed. The resolutions had been worked out behind the scenes of the official Church position by individual critical scholars. Preeminent among them was M.-J. Lagrange.

Lagrange was a contemporary of Loisy and, like Loisy, he was committed to critical study of the Bible. Because of the strong passions of the period, Lagrange was sometimes attacked as a Modernist. But Lagrange assumed fundamentally different stands on the critical issues. On the relationship of criticism to the *Magisterium*, Lagrange differed sharply with Loisy. Loisy held to a completely unfettered criticism, a direct threat to the Church's control of its own theology. Lagrange, by contrast, always and sincerely subordinated critical work to the theological judgment of the Church. But, equally important, Lagrange recognized the Church's claim to authority over criticism as a theoretical premise of criticism. The Church had a right to reject criticism incompatible with its teachings and in doing so, it did not deny the validity of critical methods but asserted a higher source of truth. Lagrange used an example to show how one discipline could check another. If a historian had contemporary accounts from a number of witnesses placing an eclipse on a certain date, the historian would still not assert that the eclipse took place on that date if the calculations of astronomers placed it a week earlier.[24] The historical account would be corrected by information from a more certain source. The Church provided just such a check by its more certain knowledge.

---

23 Keith D. Stephenson, "Roman Catholic Biblical Scholarship: Its Ecclesiastical Context in the Past Hundred Years," *Encounter* 33/34 (1972), pp. 317-318.

24 M.-J. Lagrange, "Le Décret *Lamentabili Sane Exitu* et la critique historique," *RB* 16 (1907), p. 549.

Lagrange's position expressed an attitude and a *regula* for the relation of the Church to criticism. It did not specifically address the epistemological problems in combining scientific knowledge with
knowledge given by revelation; it simply stated an essential rule governing priority and thereby allowed criticism to move back within the
Church. For its part the Church was careful not to force the epistemological issue. Lagrange stressed the almost total absence of points
on which the *Magisterium* or the unanimous witness of the Fathers had
mandated a position in opposition to criticism.[25] With these few exceptions, the scholar had complete freedom. Practically, the question was
moot. The critic and his research were in theory under the authority of
the Church. But the Church in the past had seldom exercised its
authority and, increasingly, was too prudent to do so.

Lagrange further pursued a way around the most serious problem,
that criticism seemed continually to imply error in the Bible and thus
to undermine its authority. Lagrange centered the discussion of this
most recalcitrant problem on the doctrine of inspiration and particularly the human element in it. Lagrange did not, however, subscribe
to the simplest solution, that the truth in Scripture was God's, the error
the human author's. This solution was cut off by *Providentissimus Deus*,
as we have seen. Lagrange actually followed another section of
Providentissimus Deus. Speaking of biblical reports of physical facts,
Leo XIII had argued that the biblical authors had simply gone by appearances, reporting physical phenomena as they appeared to them,
not according to modern scientific standards of accuracy. No sophistry
was involved in maintaining that in such cases the Bible was not in error
despite differences with scientific explanations. The Pope goes on to
say, "The principles here laid down will apply to cognate sciences, and
especially to history."[26]

But what were the principles involved? Lagrange worked them out,
beginning with a point of Thomistic logic. Truth and falsity are proper-
ties of formal propositions only.[27] If the sacred author did not intend
to make a proposition about a historical event, the text was neither true
nor false. "It's very simple. A proposition is true or false, but here there

25 M.-J. Lagrange, "L'interpretation de la Sainte Ecriture par l'Eglise,"
RB 9 (1900), p. 140.
26 Pope Leo XIII, *Providentissimus Deus* in Megivern, *Bible Interpretation*,
p. 214; also cf. D & S 3290.
27 M.-J. Lagrange, *La méthode historique*, edition augmentée (Paris:
Librairie Victor Lecoffre, 1904), p. 105.

is no proposition."[28] The whole issue turned on the intentions of the author; if the author did not express a judgment as to fact that could be either true or false, truth or falsity was not an issue. Lagrange redirected the truth question away from a strict calculation whether the words of the text corresponded to what actually happened by intervening the prior question whether any truth claim was being made by the author. This logical distinction, which sounds very modern, was extremely important because it avoided the imputation of error to the Bible. Lagrange based the argument that the human author often did not intend to make a strictly historical or scientific proposition on three considerations. First, following *Providentissimus Deus*, Lagrange argued that the authors had gone by sensible appearances and had no knowledge of, and therefore no intent to make, scientific formulations in a modern sense. Neither did they aim at modern standards of historical accuracy, but simply preserved the memory of their nation.

Secondly, Lagrange argued that it was not the intent of the inspired authors to record "that which is not useful for our salvation," in St. Augustine's words.[29] The primary intent, which was supported by inspiration, was to convey God's teaching which had been revealed. Augustine's principle did not mean that those elements of the text which were strictly profane were not written under inspiration. Lagrange was at pains to avoid any division of the canon into inspired and uninspired. The whole canon was inspired, but inspired toward its goal of passing on revelation, not toward reporting inconsequential detail. The narratives and accounts of the Bible are instrumental in achieving the primary goal of conveying revealed teaching, but they are not ends in themselves, as when the author makes a formal proposition about history.

Thirdly, Lagrange introduced the concept of genre as a gauge of the author's intentions. A formal historical proposition might occur in royal annals or other genres of historical reportage and then it would exhibit an appropriate form. Historical accounts with this form do in fact occur with some frequency in the Bible. But there are many other passages testifying to numerous other genres: psalms, proverbs, parables, and so on. "Each must be interpreted according to its rules."[30] It was a false step to force the whole Bible into the logic appropriate to one genre because then one missed what the author in-

---

28 Ibid.
29 Ibid., p. 88.
30 Ibid., p. 94.

tended to say. Again, Lagrange's caution against mixing categories has a very modern sound.

Lagrange's major hermeneutical contribution was to move the author to the center of interpretation. But the author was not the object of interest in his own right. The interpretive task was not to establish a personal union of spirit with the author, as in Schleiermacher's hermeneutics. The author for Lagrange was the inspired instrument by which revelation was conveyed to the Church. The emphasis fell on what the author intended to say, in which could be found the inspired testimony to divine revelation. In determining what the author intended, criticism could be of much practical use in specifying the genre used, the circumstances in which the author wrote, the situation addressed. In all cases the interpretive task was to determine what the author had put into the text.

By introducing the author's intentions into the discussion, Lagrange lowered the intensity of the debate on inerrancy. But Lagrange did not resolve the problem of inerrancy by sacrificing the relevance of the texts. The whole of Scripture was not direct revelation; this was simply a fact and not a judgment on authority. If Scripture were revelation *in toto*, a book that dropped from heaven, there would be no way around the problems raised by even trivial discrepancies. But Scripture was not revelation but the inspired witness to revelation. Revelation took place through the history of Israel and in the life of Christ, and Scripture was the normative witness to that revelation. The normative character of that witness was adequately grounded in the inspiration of Scripture. The Bible was therefore indispensable because it alone provided inspired access to revelation.

Although but little reflected in official Church pronouncements made during his lifetime, Lagrange's influence was enormous. His personal example of piety and submission, coming from the most prominent Catholic biblical scholar, created an atmosphere in which criticism could move out from under its cloud of suspicion. Lagrange's influence is most apparent in other critical scholars. Nowhere is that influence more obvious than in Franz von Hummelauer, a prominent German scholar contemporary with Lagrange. Von Hummelauer's early career was as a rationalizing apologist for a naively realistic reading of the Bible. Lagrange himself did not know quite what to make of von Hummelauer's explanation that Lot's wife had fallen into the Dead

Sea in her haste to escape Sodom, coating herself with its famous salt.[31] But, by 1904 von Hummelauer had read Lagrange's *La méthode historique* and recognized the importance of its principles. There is a remarkable transformation in von Hummelauer's own book, *Exegetisches zur Inspirationsfrage*, a work that continually cites Lagrange and the *Revue Biblique*, while going beyond Lagrange exegetically in the matter of genres and the importance of the author. As Lagrange's principles spread among scholars such as von Hummelauer, they provided the background against which a more liberal attitude toward criticism could emerge.

Lagrange's greatest influence, ultimately, was on *Divino Afflante Spiritu* itself. It is Lagrange's principles that are sanctioned in the encyclical. Lagrange's broader recognition of the human element in Scripture is reflected in the opening paragraph of *Divino Afflante Spiritu* when compared to *Providentissimus Deus* of fifty years earlier. *Providentissimus* began, "The God of all Providence...has bestowed upon man a splendid gift and safeguard." *Divino Afflante Spiritu* begins its considerations with man. "Inspired by the Divine spirit, the Sacred Writers composed those books, which God...deigned to bestow on them." The shift in emphasis toward the human author is explicit in paragraphs thirty-three and thirty-four.

> Let the interpreter then, with all care and without neglecting any light derived from recent research, endeavor to determine the peculiar character and circumstances of the sacred writer, the age in which he lived, the sources written or oral to which he had recourse and the forms of expression he employed.
>
> Thus can be better understood who was the inspired author, and what he wishes to express by his writing. There is no one indeed but knows that the supreme rule of interpretation is to discover and define what the author intended.[32]

This "supreme rule of interpretation" had not always been so self-evident and, in fact, this formulation obscures a definite hermeneutical shift that needs to be seen plainly. This hermeneutical shift involved the literal sense and it emerges in paragraph twenty-three of the encyclical:

> Being thoroughly prepared by the knowledge of the ancient languages and by the aids afforded by the art of criticism, let the Catholic exegete undertake the task, of all those imposed on him the greatest, that, namely, of dis-

---

31 Ibid., p. 203.
32 Pope Pius XII, *Divino Afflante Spiritu* in Megivern, *Bible Interpretation*, p. 331.

covering and expounding the genuine meaning of the Sacred Books. In the performance of this task let the interpreters bear in mind that their foremost and greatest endeavor should be to discern and define clearly that sense of the biblical words which is called literal. Aided by the context and by comparison with similar passages, let them therefore by means of their knowledge of language search out with all diligence the literal meaning of the words; all these helps indeed are wont to be pressed into service in the explanation also of profane writers, so that the mind of the author may be made abundantly clear.[33]

The innovation is contained in the last clause. It is the equation of the literal sense with the mind of the author in this paragraph and the instruction contained in paragraph thirty-five to use critical tools to ascertain the author's intent that marks the new hermeneutical emphasis characteristic of *Divino Afflante Spiritu*. For Aquinas to know the plain literal sense of a text immediately was to know the author's intent. In *Divino Afflante Spiritu* the direction in which one moves is reversed. One must first know the intent to know the meaning. The exegete proceeds through the text to the source of meaning behind it. When the hermeneutical task is construed in this way, there is a quite obvious role for criticism in establishing the author's intent and, consequently, the meaning. Exegesis is a discovery process by which an object that is not immediately obvious, the meaning, is found. Information secured by critical study is the key to successful discovery.

At the same time the emphasis on the author reduces the pressure on the issue of inerrancy. If critical research shows conclusively that the biblical text does not correspond to historical events, that fact is no longer to be taken to entail error in the Bible. In the new conception it is evidence that the author did not intend to teach a historical truth. This, of course, does not mean that the author did not intend to convey a divine truth. It is all the more likely that when the error of viewing the author as primarily a historian is corrected and his intent rightly understood, it will be seen to be to pass on the things of God, *ad doctrinam nostram scripta*. The theological truth of the Bible is not compromised by discounting historical details the author never intended to teach. The problem of inerrancy assumes manageable proportions when it is located within the larger task of determining the author's intentions.

There is a sense in which every encyclical or pronouncement looks backward to issues of the preceding period. This is certainly true of *Divino Afflante Spiritu*. The issues it resolved had been raised fifty years

33 Ibid., p. 327; also cf. D & S 3826.

earlier in the Modernist crisis. The nature of those issues made *Divino Afflante Spiritu* a very narrow document, despite the revolutionary impact it had on the direction of Catholic exegesis. The pressure in the Modernist period was toward the acceptance of critical methods. That pressure was irresistible if the Church were to be a twentieth-century institution. The primary barriers to the acceptance of criticism were the issues of inerrancy, with its challenge to scriptural authority, and the subordination of criticism to the Church, the denial of which challenged Church authority. The broader hermeneutical issues of how the text was actually to be used in the twentieth-century Church were largely submerged beneath the preoccupation with removing these barriers on one side and an unreflective assumption that critical information was valuable and applicable in its own right on the other. In any case the spirit of the age demanded a critical posture. When, therefore, the narrow issues blocking the way were resolved or at least the tension reduced, Pius XII opened the door and critical scholarship entered, yet without a clear sense of where it was going next. Critical programs for research were in place, but the necessary hermeneutical reflection on how those programs contributed to the better understanding or full use of Scripture had barely begun.

The encyclical contained within itself the seeds of the next generation of issues. It did not resolve the question of the relation of the critical understanding of the sense of the text to the traditional understanding held by the Church Fathers and the Church's most eminent theologians of the precritical age, a sense reflected in traditional belief and practice. If anything, the acceptance of criticism intensified the problem. In *Divino Afflante Spiritu* the meaning of the text is understood as a single thing, an object created and transmitted to the text by its author. Using the methods of critical scholarship, it is possible to reconstruct the author's intentions and hence the meaning. The conflict with traditional understandings of the meaning of the text arises almost inevitably because the Church Fathers, for instance, based their exegesis on radically different hermeneutical principles and employed other methodologies than modern exegetes. There are no obvious points of contact between the hermeneutical principles of Irenaeus and Roland de Vaux. Nor is there any easy way simply to ignore the problem. Both traditional exegesis and modern critical exegesis claim at least implicitly to define the same thing, the literal sense of the text. Yet both cannot be correct if that sense is a single thing, an assumption nearly all Catholic exegetes share and an implication of

Divino Afflante Spiritu's identification of the literal sense with the author's intentions. Under these circumstances traditional exegesis is at a severe disadvantage. In the twentieth century it is a general assumption that the way to gain knowledge of any object, not excepting the meaning of a text, is to apply the critical methodologies appropriate to the nature of the particular object. The conflict between the traditional understanding of the sense of the text and the modern understanding resolves itself into a matter of epistemology. Modern criticism marshalls the methods recognized today as appropriate to the textual object, while traditional understandings of Scripture rest on principles no longer recognized as valid. In a direct confrontation of this sort, modern criticism must win out, though it is a Pyrrhic victory. The imperialism of critical epistemology overwhelms all earlier exegesis.

Nor did *Divino Afflante Spiritu* put to rest the question of the irrelevance of the meaning which criticism itself discovered. The encyclical confidently assumed that when the author's intentions were seen clearly, they would be theologically relevant. Indeed they would appear as the divinely revealed premises required for theological argumentation in the scholastic mode. Criticism would strip away the inessential historical details without disturbing the theological truth in Scripture. It was not difficult to concede the historical details because they were not considered significant in themselves. Remove them and the theological teachings would stand out the more clearly.

Loisy had already recognized the danger of this approach in his attack on Harnack. When one considers the text from the outset as a historical object, as modern critics have, everything about it appears historically conditioned. There is no pure theological residuum. The deepest theological teachings of the Bible emerge from historical investigation as the response of a particular community to a particular situation, not as revealed timeless truths. There is nothing nefarious in this; it is the inevitable result of viewing the text historically. The types of irrelevancy represented by both Loisy and Harnack creep in as the meaning of the text is placed more firmly in relation to a fixed historical context which is now remote.

The critics' natural propensity to focus on matters that their methodologies are best suited to investigate raises a related problem. Timeless theological truths are not subject to historical study. They would require a set of methodologies to reveal them which the historical critic does not control and might not even recognize. Criticism therefore turns to more accessible matters of a more appropriately historical character such as the background of the author, the sociological setting of the biblical community, the material culture of Iron Age III, and so on. Research, though in a sense still about the biblical text, becomes more esoteric, more loosely affiliated with the text and with the theological interest which dominates the Church's relationship to the Bible. Critical studies become mere preliminaries to the true theological task of exegesis. *Divino Afflante Spiritu* warned against the aridity that can displace theological exegesis but did not provide adequate principles to combat it.[34] Moving through the text to what lies behind it provides new knowledge, but not necessarily nourishment, to sustain the life of the Church.

Divino Afflante Spiritu did not anticipate the full range of new problems that consistent application of critical methodologies to the Bible would bring. It supposed the Modernist beast domesticated. But historical criticism has proven difficult to harness to the work of the Church. The limits of historical criticism have, in the period since *Divino Afflante Spiritu*, set a new task for exegetes. The hermeneutical discussion of how Scripture is understood and used has had to be broadened. *Divino Afflante Spiritu* climaxed the restricted discussion of whether criticism could be brought within the Church and on what terms. Since the encyclical, critical study has been a given in the hermeneutical discussion. By accepting criticism, the encyclical settled the narrow issue that had long preoccupied exegetes and channeled the hermeneutical discussion. It therefore created the preconditions for an expanded hermeneutical discussion and, paradoxically, as the limitations of the historical methods it sanctioned became apparent, it also created the need for it. The hermeneutical reflection now possible can go beyond the point represented by *Divino Afflante Spiritu* to broaden its perspective to include the full range of ways in which Scripture has functioned in the Church in the past and continues to function today. Scripture continues to shape personal belief, to direct the efforts of the Church to articulate its relationship to God, to unite the community of believers with each other and with the faithful of the past, and to enrich the solemn practice of worship and devotion of the community of faith. It is the power of Scripture to speak and to direct the faithful to God, a power everywhere visible within the community of faith, which is the appropriate subject of hermeneutical discussion in the period after *Divino Afflante Spiritu*.

---

34 Ibid., p. 328; also cf. D & S 3826-3828.

Chapter 2

Sensus Plenior

In 1925 when Andrés Fernández first coined the term *sensus plenior*, opposition to critical scholarship still represented the official Church position.[1] The encyclical letter *Spiritus Paraclitus* of Pope Benedict XV (September 15, 1920) on the fifteenth centenary of Saint Jerome continued the anticritical proscriptions of the anti-Modernist decrees and even closed some of the loopholes in earlier encyclicals which might have encouraged critics.[2] It would be a mistake, however, to conclude that the attitude of the official documents accurately reflected the position of Catholic biblical scholars. The influence of moderate critical scholars such as Lagrange was immense and, behind the scenes, they quietly revolutionized the assumptions of Catholic biblical scholarship. The tide toward historical criticism which finally broke over the Church in *Divino Afflante Spiritu* was already rising.

The assumption common to all scholars who adopted critical methods in this period was that the literal sense would only yield itself to historical research. This assumption followed from a new understanding of the literal sense. As Lagrange, for instance, understood it, the literal sense was a fixed form of the intentions of the author. Sense was primarily a function of the author rather than the text itself. In determining the sense, then, the inquiry naturally shifted from the text to the author. The author became the determiner of meaning, and the issue of the fundamental nature of the author or, more broadly, of all human existence, became a part of the question about the sense of the

---

1 Andrés Fernández, "Hermeneutica," *Institutiones Biblicae* (Rome: Pontifical Biblical Institute, 1925), I, pp. 390-391.

2 Pope Benedict XV, *Spiritus Paraclitus* in Megivern, *Bible Interpretation*, pp. 267-302; also cf. D & S 3650-3654.

text. Although there was not a single anthropological theory shared by all Catholic scholars even tacitly, there was an underlying agreement that the fundamental character of human existence was shaped and directed by historical circumstances. The sacred authors were subject to this fundamentally historical nature of existence no less than all other people. Their intentions, therefore, in writing their books were subject to the same historical contingency. The literal sense of the sacred books was therefore also a historically determined object and fell within the province of historical research. Historical criticism enjoyed an exclusive franchise to discover the literal sense because of its historical nature, a nature rooted in the historicity of the author.

Fernández's introduction of the *sensus plenior* in 1925 tacitly acknowledged the new situation. The literal sense was within the domain of the historical critic. The *sensus plenior* represented an effort to define a separate sense of Scripture which would not conflict with historical criticism but which could encompass traditional interpretations and preserve their claim to the inherent authority of Scripture. The *sensus plenior* is a stepchild of the critical movement. This is clear from the parallel development of the two. Fernández defined the *sensus plenior* just as the critical methods replaced precritical among the majority of scholars.[3] But the greatest interest in the *sensus plenior* came in the late 1940's through mid-1960's, after *Divino Afflante Spiritu* sanctioned critical scholarship and a new generation of critically trained scholars began to subject every quarter of the Bible to critical examination. The results of the now respectable critical investigations called into question the status of important traditional interpretations. Many Catholic scholars turned to the *sensus plenior* as a way to have both the rigor of the critical methods and the deeply rooted and theologically important precritical interpretations. Both Joseph Coppens and Raymond E. Brown, the foremost spokesmen in Europe and America, respectively, for the *sensus plenior,* recognized the connec-

---

3 Fernández's use of the concept of a more than literal sense had precedents. Lagrange wrote in 1900 of a sense "supra-littéral" which in many respects anticipated the *sensus plenior* ("L'interprétation," pp. 141-142).

tion between the rise of critical methodology and the emergence of the *sensus plenior*:

> ...it is a theological sense...it serves above all to close the hiatus which, in certain matters, threatens to be produced between the sources of revelation and the present doctrine of the Church.[4]

> A very important factor that explains the popularity of the theory has been its usefulness in winning in the Church a tolerance for the historical-critical exegesis of the Bible. In the 1930s and 1940s it was becoming more and more obvious to Catholic scholars that the traditional exegesis of the Bible (patristic, liturgical, theological) did not agree in many points with modern critical exegesis.[5]

The apologetic origins of the *sensus plenior* must be registered fully. *Sensus plenior* did not develop from broad and systematic hermeneutical reflection. Its shape was narrowly circumscribed by two apologetic requirements. It had to be compatible with historical criticism and it had to allow room for traditional exegesis. Not surprisingly, the theory of a *sensus plenior* mirrors very closely the hermeneutical assumptions underlying much of Catholic critical scholarship in this period. Most importantly, it shares the fundamental assumption that the sense of the text is a function of the author's intentions. This assumption, in fact, becomes the key to the *sensus plenior*. Scripture is unlike all other texts in that it is formed by two authors simultaneously. Two consciousnesses — that of God and the human author — cooperate in the production of Scripture. The theory of the *sensus plenior* seizes on the possibility that God's intentions diverge or exceed those of the human author, creating elements of meaning beyond what the human author intended. The human author addressed the contemporary situation and, under inspiration, directed the literal sense of his words to it. This sense falls properly within the realm of critical scholarship. But God, acting in strict analogy to the human author, created additional meaning. The *sensus plenior* is that which was intended by God beyond the

---

4 Joseph Coppens, "Nouvelles réflexions sur les divers sens des Saintes Ecritures," *NRT* 74 (1952), p. 15.

5 Raymond E. Brown, "The Problems of the *Sensus Plenior*," *ETL* 43/3-4 (1967), p. 460.

literal intentions of the human author. Raymond Brown's definition of
the *sensus plenior* states the relationship concisely:

> The *sensus plenior* is that additional meaning, intended by God but not clear-
> ly intended by the human author, which is seen to exist in the words of a bibli-
> cal text (or group of texts, or even a whole book) when they are studied in
> the light of further revelation or development in the understanding of revela-
> tion.[6]

By locating the additional meaning that constitutes the *sensus plenior* initially in the consciousness of God, the theory removes it from historical critical scrutiny. God's consciousness is not bounded by historical circumstances in the same way as the human author's. One apologetic aim is met. But at the same time, placing the meaning in such an inaccessible realm raises very serious questions about how we know the added meaning and how it can be demonstrated in a fashion sufficiently rigorous to satisfy the critical temperament. Even the human consciousness in which the literal sense is created is a mysterious region not open to direct scrutiny. Historical criticism under the most optimistic interpretation draws inferences and analogies about what the words in the text meant to the author, given the historical situation in which the text was composed. Even in the human sphere, the discovery of meaning according to this theory is problematic. When the consciousness that is the key to meaning is God's, the problems are compounded. The mind of God is a region even less accessible than the mind of a human author. Theologians have never ventured to define it in more than vague comparisons with human minds. The *sensus plenior* acquires room for additional meaning in the text, it seems, only by pushing the analogy between the human and divine authors to the breaking point. One must either accept that the *sensus plenior* is unknowable, locked in God's consciousness, or lose all control over the range of meaning claimed in the text. Any suggested interpretation could claim to represent God's intentions with equal probability, since God's intentions cannot be summoned directly to adjudicate the matter.

Brown is sensitive both to the danger of opening the floodgates to claims for Spiritual authority for all sorts of radical interpretations and

6 Raymond E. Brown, *The Sensus Plenior of Sacred Scripture* (Baltimore: St. Mary's University Press, 1955), p. 92.

the apologetic need to maintain strict controls in order to insure critical acceptance of the theory. Continuing the analogy to critical scholarship, Brown demands that there be external evidence of God's having intended the *sensus plenior*. But only further revelation could count as evidence of God's consciousness. There is no independent and objective route to God's intentions except what God publicly reveals. In practice, only authoritative sources such as the authors of the New Testament, the Fathers, and the *Magisterium* of the Church which have a privileged access to God's revelation can supply additional evidence of God's intentions. The author of Matthew 1:23, for instance, testifies by the formulation of that verse to a revelation that Isaiah 7:14, "Behold a virgin shall conceive," was intended by God to refer to Mary. That reference goes beyond the intention of the human author. The understanding of Isaiah 7:14 in Matthew 1:23, since it was formed under inspiration, stands as evidence of the actual meaning intended in Isaiah 7:14.

The demand for evidence completes the analogy to critical scholarship. Discovering the *sensus plenior* is a matter of sufficient evidence. Consistently, the evidence is of a type appropriate to the object to be established — God's intentions.

The demand for evidence of God's intentions answers very well requirements placed on the theory by critical scholarship. The line of argument replicates the *a posteriori* mode of objective scientific inquiry from evidence to conclusion. Brown can base his argument on an observation that cannot be denied by the most skeptical critic, the fact that the New Testament and the Fathers see additional meaning in the Old Testament text beyond what critical scholars would consider the literal sense. From that objective observation it is possible to argue that the meaning was intended by God and is therefore in the text. The form of the argument is similar to critical argumentation. Further, by limiting evidence to authoritative sources, Brown eliminated novel and uncontrolled interpretations. The perceptions of modern scholars, no matter how profound theologically, cannot claim the direct authority of Scripture because they were not included in the original intentions of God. The *sensus plenior* is limited to already existing interpretations by authoritative individuals or, possibly, to the results of new revelation given through the proper channels of the *Magisterium*. This principle of exclusivity also keeps exegetes in the appropriate objective, descriptive mode with regard to Scripture. Their task is not to innovate new meaning but strictly to discover the meaning to which the New Testament and Fathers bear witness.

The demand that there be revealed evidence of the *sensus plenior* of a biblical text provides an important criterion but in itself is not sufficient. There are many instances of fanciful interpretations both in the New Testament and in the writings of the Fathers. One would not want to be required to accept all of them as the sense of Scripture simply because an inspired writer had written them. To protect against overextension, Brown introduced a second criterion. The *sensus plenior* must be a homogeneous development of the literal sense. The name of the sense itself implies this criterion. The *sensus plenior* is fuller, not different.[7]

Brown does not define homogeneous development in the dissertation, and that lack of definition presents a problem in conceiving the relation between the *sensus plenior* and the literal sense. Nonetheless, the apologetic effect of the criterion is absolutely clear. It harnesses the *sensus plenior* to the lead horse of the literal sense. To be able to establish homogeneity as an argument for the *sensus plenior*, the exegete must first establish the literal sense. The priority of the literal sense receives explicit recognition in the process of identifying an instance of *sensus plenior*.

The core of the theory of *sensus plenior* is remarkably simple and easily summarized. It is based on a mentalistic theory of meaning in which meaning is initially a mental entity which exists properly in the mind of its author. Critical scholars preempted the investigation of what lay in the mind of the human author. Much of what was traditionally held to be the sense of the text could not be located among the author's intentions by critical methods. To explain the existence of the additional meaning represented by traditional interpretations required only the identification of another consciousness capable of creating it. The traditional metaphysical affirmation that God was the author of Scripture was taken literally and technically, so that God's consciousness was pressed into service as an explanation for the block of meaning known as the *sensus plenior*. The fundamental question of how meaning could exist in excess of what the human author intended

---

7 Ibid., p. 145.

was construed as a causal question of how a mental entity was created, and the question was answered by reference to God's consciousness. Much of the rest of the theory is not dependent on this theoretical core but on the need to assure compatibility with historical critical premises. The criterion that the *sensus plenior* be homogeneous with the literal sense explicitly recognizes the preeminence of the literal sense and the critical methods which discover it. Nothing in the basic premise of two consciousnesses requires this criterion. The added meaning formulated in God's consciousness alone could be quite different from the meaning inspired in the human without violating the concept of two consciousnesses. Likewise, the demand for evidence of God's added intentions follows criticism's empirical, *a posteriori* approach rather than the *a priori* assumptions held by precritical exegesis of what God must have intended. The *a posteriori* argumentation conforms formally to criticism but nonetheless avoids the theological limitations of the historicist view by insisting that the evidence considered be appropriate to the object being investigated, in this case, God's consciousness. Both of these criteria serve to rule out theological innovations or "spiritual" readings which would offend the critical sensibility.

The theory of a *sensus plenior* has received a great deal of attention, some of it critical. Despite the efforts to make *sensus plenior* fully compatible with critical scholarship, some critical scholars such as Bruce Vawter and John L. McKenzie in this country worried that the *sensus plenior* represented a retreat from the gains made by critical scholarship.[8] Their protest was less against specific arguments in favor of the *sensus plenior* than that the whole movement represented a diversion of attention from more important critical work on the literal sense. There was also a fear that *sensus plenior* was an attempt to sneak in the back door the "pneumatic" interpretation *Divino Afflante Spiritu* had ushered out the front. General reservations of this type are less interesting for our purposes than specific challenges to aspects of the theory. They do raise, however, a serious question whether the sensus plenior can maintain its standing within the critical framework. It will

---

8 Bruce Vawter, "The Fuller Sense: Some Considerations," *CBQ* 26 (1964), pp. 85-96; John L. McKenzie, "Problems of Hermeneutics in Roman Catholic Exegesis," *JBL* 77 (1958), pp. 197-204.

be important to return to this question after considering more specific challenges.

The question arose whether or not the human author was aware of the *sensus plenior*. Initially, the issue seems to be limited to the proper classification of the *sensus plenior*. If the human author was aware of the *sensus plenior*, he included it in his intentions and the *sensus plenior* falls within the broad bounds of the literal sense. If the author was not aware of it, a separate classification is appropriate. In his dissertation Brown used the formulation "intended by God but not clearly intended by the human author" to hedge on the issue.[9] In further discussion within the dissertation, Brown is clearly less interested in the human author's consciousness than in that of God, which actually defines the *sensus plenior*. In his next article on the subject after the dissertation, "The *Sensus Plenior* in the Last Ten Years," he attempts to bracket out the question of the author's intentions entirely.[10]

If the issue were simply proper classification, no one would dispute the propriety of ruling it out. But the issue lies deeper within the theory, nearer its heart, though I am not sure that Brown realized it. The theory of the *sensus plenior* holds that a determinate mental entity is created by God's consciousness. That entity must be transmitted to the text, which is produced concretely by a human author, acting under inspiration. The *sensus plenior* meaning must pass in some fashion through the consciousness of the human author and some account must be given of the mechanism by which this takes place if there is not to be a damaging lacuna in the theory.

The circumstances of the formation of the literal sense are relatively comprehensible. It is true that the precise mechanism of inspiration

---

9 Brown, *Sensus Plenior of Sacred Scripture*, p. 92.
10 Raymond E. Brown, "The *Sensus Plenior* in the Last Ten Years," *CBQ* 25 (1963).

is obscure. Only those who have been inspired could have introspective knowledge of it. But the general process of the creation of meaning seems accessible introspectively to each individual;[11] we all engage
in creating meaning even if we could not articulate a full account of the
process involved. But the process of transmission of meaning formed
by one individual within meaning created by another is obscure because no single analogy covers it.

Rudolph Bierberg, who is opposed to the *sensus plenior*, considered
two traditionally recognized methods, inspiration and direction revelation, by which God controlled the meaning finally embodied in Scripture.[12] Neither admits the *sensus plenior*. In the case of direct
revelation, as when a prophet directly delivers God's words with the
formula, "Thus says the Lord," the human author's consciousness does
not participate in the creation of meaning. The author is the passive
channel of revelation. Under these circumstances only one consciousness is involved and there is only one meaning in the text. The meaning revealed through the prophet is the literal sense.[13] Considering the
author's consciousness passive does not open a channel for the *sensus
plenior* but rather makes the sense of the text completely univocal. Only
one consciousness participates; only one sense results.

In the first case, if one supposes that the human author was completely passive, then revelation is the proper category and there is only
one sense in the text, the literal. If one supposes that the human author
was actively involved, the correct category is inspiration. In inspiration
God directs the creative processes of the author's mind which actually produce the sense. If the meaning which constitutes the sensus
plenior were already fixed by God's consciousness, then this
mechanism of inspiration which uses the author's mental powers would

---

11 There are problems associated with this simple assumption of
introspective knowledge of the working of our minds ranging from
psychological (the Freudian emphasis on the unconscious) to logical (all we
see on introspection is the result of thought, not thought itself). Neither
Brown nor his critics register the difficulties but work within what is
essentially a Thomistic psychology.
12 Rudolph Bierberg, "Does Sacred Scripture Have a *Sensus Plenior*?"
CBQ 10 (1948), pp. 182-195.
13 Ibid., pp. 189-192.

be by-passed. The theory of the *sensus plenior* forces a paradox. If there were a *sensus plenior*, it would not be inspired.[14] Inspiration requires that sense be created in the mind of the human author. God inspires by directing that process. For Bierberg, then, either of the possible suppositions about the author's consciousness, that it was actively or passively involved, does not allow a *sensus plenior*.

Bierberg's objection that the *sensus plenior* contradicts the nature of inspiration is echoed by Gaston Courtade, but Courtade complements Bierberg's argument by attacking the inadequate conception of the instrumentality of the human author in the theory:

> The authors were the instruments of the Holy Spirit, and Scripture proceeds integrally from it. But they were intelligent and free instruments; and Scripture, *content and form, ideas and words, thoughts and phrases,* also proceed from their intelligence and will. We may therefore not submit it to a sort of vivisection in seeking, on one hand, the sense the sacred writers have given it and on the other hand, or in addition, the sense which God has deposited unknown to them.[15]

Preformed knowledge simply passing through the human author denies the natural character of the instrument, which is to be a sentient, intelligent creator of meaning. Courtade objects that the instrument cannot be used contrary to its proper character, yet the *sensus plenior* seems to demand this by-passing of the faculties of intelligence which characterize human beings.

Both Bierberg and Courtade use different concepts drawn from scholastic theology to formulate the same charge. There is no conceivable mechanism of transmission of the *sensus plenior* which does not reduce the human author to a cypher. That is, there is no acceptable definition of the human author's role in the theory. Both Bierberg and Courtade therefore reject the *sensus plenior*.

Initially, Brown responded to the objections in two ways. First, he attacked both the arguments from inspiration and instrumentality as too *a priori* and rigid.[16] Both implied a limitation on God's freedom of action incompatible with God's essential freedom. God's action as un-

---

14 Ibid., pp. 185-189.

15 Gaston Courtade, "Les Ecritures ont-elles un sens 'plénier'?" *Recherches des Science Religieuse* 37 (1950), p. 486.

16 Brown, *Sensus Plenior of Sacred Scripture*, pp. 130, 133, 137.

created principal cause is not limited by the nature of the instruments God chooses to use.[17]

One is tempted to respond, "Well, of course, but..." to this sort of argument. God can do anything the argument requires God to do. But this sort of final appeal to God's sovereign freedom only serves to illustrate the weakness of framing the issues by reference to God's intentions. The true issue of the human mechanism is lost to sight in the speculation about what God can and cannot do.

Brown's response goes beyond ruling the critics out of court as too *a priori*. His second approach is to define the state of consciousness appropriate to the *sensus plenior*. The author's awareness cannot be complete or the *sensus plenior* becomes equivalent to the literal sense and enters the realm governed by critical methodologies. Nor can the author be completely unaware or there is no description of a mechanism which actually involves the author's faculties. Brown therefore posits a third alternative, vague awareness, which threads its way between Scylla and Charybdis.[18]

There are several ways to account for this vague awareness and therefore several ways to account for the human author's participation in the *sensus plenior*.[19] Origen suggested that prophets received a form of divine illumination which transported them out of their current situation to direct perception of divine mysteries. Brown is somewhat skeptical of this explanation; there is little evidence that this sort of illumination was given.[20] In any case, presumably the vision would give complete awareness and, therefore, the account of the vision would constitute the literal sense.

Brown is more favorably disposed toward the Antiochene hypothesis called *theoria*. The human author received divine assistance

---

17 Ibid., p. 132.

18 In his definition of the *sensus plenior* in his dissertation, Brown carefully avoids the question of the author's awareness because the *sensus plenior* is defined by God's intentions. As far as the definition is concerned, the author may be aware or unaware. See pages 105-106 of *Sensus Plenior of Sacred Scripture*. It is only on the peripheral issue of the human author's involvement that vague awareness is discussed.

19 Brown follows the discussion of Joseph Coppens, *Les Harmonies des deux testaments* (Tournai and Paris: Casterman, 1949), pp. 48-51.

20 Brown, *Sensus Plenior of Sacred Scripture*, p. 108.

to see in present events the shape of future saving acts. The author then formulated in clear language a message for his own time, but with an eye also on the future course of events. The intuition of the future given the author is not complete and fully detailed, so that the *sensus plenior* is also not obvious in the author's own time. The *sensus plenior* only unfolds as the events the author dimly foresaw actually occur.

Although the psychological events involved in *theoria* are more plausible than Origen's divine illumination, the quantity of direct evidence available to support the actual occurrence of such events is similarly small. Critical scholars, at least, would demand additional evidence. It is also difficult to imagine how *theoria* would operate in individual cases. What did the author of the *Protevangelium* see, to take one frequently mentioned *sensus plenior* passage, that gave a dim awareness of the Virgin Mary's triumph over evil? Exemplified in individual cases that require one to suppose that the human author had vague foreknowledge of very specific events centuries in advance, *theoria* seems a very dubious hypothesis. Brown drops it in his next article on *sensus plenior* following his dissertation.[21]

Apart from the question of how vague awareness could be gained by the author, for which there is no satisfactory answer, is the whole question of what vague awareness is like, the definition of the concept itself. Brown uses a common enough situation to illustrate.[22] At some point we all find ourselves at a loss for words, struggling to articulate something but conscious of our failure. Then someone in our audience comes to our rescue with a concise statement. We acknowledge it with, "That's just what I had in mind." Vague awareness is like that. The human author is like the person unable to articulate his idea until God, through further revelation, provides a clear statement.

The shortcoming of this illustration, which at first seems so admirable, is that the statement, "That's just what I had in mind," is seriously misleading if it is taken as the literal report of a mental event. Brown implies that the stumbler did have an idea present in his head in some prelinguistic form but it was somewhat fuzzy. We often think

---

21 Brown, *"Sensus Plenior* in the Last Ten Years," p. 268.
22 Brown (*Sensus Plenior of Sacred Scripture*, pp. 111-112) follows Jean Gribomont, "Le Lien des deux Testaments selon la théologie de S. Thomas," *ETL* 22 (1946), pp. 84-86.

of inarticulateness as a coherent idea lacking coherent expression. But getting beyond unreflective assumptions, it is clear that confusion or vagueness is not the presence of a clear idea in incoherent form but the absence of any clear idea. Thinking is done in language, whether out loud or in our private ear. There are no ideas which precede their expression in language. When one is incoherent, what is present in his head, if we are to continue this misleading metaphor, is confusion and his talk is full and adequate expression of it. Every teacher assumes this. No one gives high marks for an incomprehensible paper on the assumption that the student had a brilliant idea but just could not get it out. The student does not understand and the essay is the expression of that misunderstanding.

The point could be argued at greater length theoretically, but it is adequate to say that we do and necessarily must assume the identity between the meaning (or lack of it) we receive from any statement and what was going on in the author's mind. There is no warrant for positing a private realm of thinking where ideas are actually formed before being given linguistic form, a two-tiered system. With remarkable candor Brown admits that the actual exegetical process assumes the identity of internal ideas and external expression:

> From some discussions of the literal sense we might get the impression that, first, one knows what the human author meant and that, therefore, one knows what a text means. Actually, the process of exegesis is the reverse: one discovers first what the text says, and then one attempts to draw from this the outlook and meaning of the author.[23]

To return to the original issue of mechanism and apply these considerations: if the human author had an incomplete or partial grasp of

---

23 Brown, "*Sensus Plenior* in the Last Ten Years," p. 263. Bruce Vawter takes vigorous exception to Brown's statement, insisting on the exegetical centrality of the author's consciousness ("Fuller Sense"). It is one of those rare ironic examples of an argument disproving itself. Vawter argues the proverbial case of a pied font of type producing a Shakespeare play on its own. In this case, Vawter argues, the play would mean absolutely nothing, because there was no consciousness to produce meaning. One dares suppose that if such a manuscript were conveyed to a literary agent, the agent would be able to make something of it even if it were not *King Lear* but only began with such a line as, "Well you know or don't kennet or haven't I told you every telling has a taling and that's the he and the she of it."

the *sensus plenior*, no matter how it was derived, what could be trans-mitted into the text would only be that incomplete idea or confusion, not a complete idea *in nuce*, nor a complete idea in incoherent form, nor the seed which will grow into the *sensus plenior*, nor any other metaphor. A confused version of the *sensus plenior* is not the *sensus plenior*.

In summary: The hypothesis of vague awareness will not serve be-cause vague awareness is incommensurate with the effect it is posited to explain: the transmission of an ultimately full and clear sense into the text. Even if it were to serve, there is no explanation of how the vague awareness would arise, since both Origen's divine illumination and Antiochene *theoria* fail for want of supporting evidence. The mechanism of the human author's involvement remains mysterious.

The failure of even these formal, *ad hoc* efforts to provide a mechanism by which the *sensus plenior* finds its way into the human author's text testifies to severe weakness in the theory. The formula-tion of both the literal sense and the *sensus plenior* as functions of the authors' consciousnesses requires specifying the coordinated activity of two independent consciousnesses. In itself, this is difficult, but the coordination must be accomplished without violating the very different individual characters of each author. The difficulties freighting this delicate task of balancing are compounded by the use of Thomistic psychological categories in which the creative faculties to be balanced are shrouded in a mysterious, prelinguistic realm of pure ideas.

The difficulties are further compounded by conceiving of meaning as a "thing," a determinate mental entity in some ways independent of its verbal expression. The reification of the meaning creates what seems to me an insurmountable difficulty in conceiving how this entity created solely by God is passed through the consciousness of the human author without violating the nature of that author's consciousness. All at-tempts to circumvent the problem must be unavailing so long as mean-ing is a fixed entity.

Uncertainties about the mechanism by which the *sensus plenior* is transmitted to the text soon raise questions whether the *sensus plenior* actually resides in the text at all. John P. Weisengoff expressed misgiv-ings about the role of the human author similar to those of Courtade in a review of *Problèmes et méthodes d'exégèse théologique*, a collection of articles by three of the most prominent European advocates of the *sensus plenior*:

> Inspired writers are human instruments, i.e., instruments endowed with intellect and will. They are true authors, however, with their activities as authors compenetrated by the influence of God, the principal author....This prompts the reviewer to reject the idea of a lack of full correspondence between what God intends and what the human author intends.[24]

The *sensus plenior* is excluded by incompatibility with the nature of the human instruments. Weisengoff follows through to the obvious concomitant that the *sensus plenior* is not *in* the original text as its sense. But Weisengoff does not argue with what we have called the *a posteriori* observation that there is additional meaning when the Old Testament is read in conjunction with the New. This is a given, but how to explain it? Weisengoff suggests that when God inspired the Old Testament, God did not intend a full revelation of the whole course of saving history, even though He was certainly aware of it. Revelation was progressive. The Old Testament authors were inspired to write only what was appropriate for their own times. Later authors at the proper moment were then inspired to provide the true and authoritative interpretation of the earlier passage:

> It will be only later that God by another revelation will add a note or notes to something already given or will clarify what was obscure; and so, what God knew but did not reveal in the former item of revelation becomes intended and revealed in the later revelation.[25]

Taking a broad view, Weisengoff's distinction between later interpretation and earlier meaning does not seem to do full justice to the fact that both texts and not just the later "interpretation" are involved in the creation of new meaning in the case of Isaiah 7:14 and Matthew 1:23, for instance. But Weisengoff's suggestion does respect the human author's full participation in the process of creating meaning and, in addition, exposes a weakness in the theory of the *sensus plenior*. One is forced by the theory to suppose that the additional meaning that constituted the *sensus plenior* passed undetected in the text for centuries. Explanations of how the added meaning remained hidden which argue for the necessity of additional revelation are possible — Brown proposes the analogy of a darkened room gradually illuminated; still,

24 John P. Weisengoff, review of *Problèmes et méthodes d'exégèse théologique*, ed. L. Cerfaux, *CBQ* 14 (1952), p. 85.
25 Ibid.

there is unease at the notion of an entity in the text that cannot be perceived. Weisengoff's theory of a later addition of meaning at least avoids this mysterious entity.

Brown's response to Weisengoff was very direct. Weisengoff formulated his objections as a question of what God intended. "The above leads us to what is really the heart of the problem. In the O.T. did God *intend*, even though at times implicitly and obscurely, to reveal the additions or the 'more' which we find in the N.T.?"[26] The issue turns on God's intentions and, given that, Brown found it very unlikely that God knew the whole course of saving history yet for some reason refrained from making it an actual part of the Old Testament passages. Brown probably gets the best of this exercise in speculation, but the only sure result of this sort of controversy is general skepticism about the whole affair. The formulation of the *sensus plenior* as a direct function of God's intentions leaves the theory particularly prey to this sort of debilitating weakness. In any case, Brown's answer does not touch the underlying unease with the mysteriously resurfacing meaning which Weisengoff taps.

In the article already mentioned, Rudolph Bierberg raises the same problem of the mode of existence of the *sensus plenior* as a problem in Thomistic logic. Bierberg's argument is highly technical and based on an Aristotelian logical system no longer widely accepted. The logical system, however, is presupposed by most writers on the *sensus plenior*, both pro and con. It provides the logical substructure of the theory and, therefore, needs to be examined.

Bierberg expects broad agreement on some general logical considerations and premises about how terms and concepts are meaningful. He cites Coffey, a logician:

> There are two kinds of signification or meaning in *most* of our ideas and terms. A concept or term *applies to* or *stands for* an object or class of objects, and it implies certain attributes which the objects possess in common.[27]

Bierberg goes on, "The sense of a word, therefore, is the comprehension and extension of the idea which it expresses — or what is the same

26 Ibid., p. 84.
27 Peter Coffey, *The Science of Logic* (New York: Peter Smith, 1938), I, p. 43, quoted in Bierberg, "Does Sacred Scripture?," p.183.

thing, its connotation and denotation, its content and application."[28]
This is familiar idealistic theory, in which the true sense of terms or
concepts properly lies in the reality which lies behind them, in the object to which a term refers and the attributes which that object possesses.

At this point Bierberg introduces a distinction crucial to the rest of
his argument. The "comprehension" of a term has two aspects, objective and subjective. The objective comprehension is "the sum-total of
all the attributes *de facto* common to the objects referred to, whether
these attributes be known or not."[29] The subjective comprehension
represents a subset, "the sum-total of attributes brought up before the
mind of any individual by the presence in his mind of the concept expressed by the term in question...This quantity is essentially variable
from individual to individual."[30]

A simple example will illustrate the distinction. The objective comprehension of the term "tree" contains all the attributes de facto applicable to the thing "tree": woody stem, major root system, height,
branchiness, leaves, and so on. The subjective comprehension would
be much narrower and include only those attributes an individual intended to be included in any particular instance of use of the term. An
individual referring to a young tree would include roots, branches, and
leaves but not height. Someone speaking of a family tree would only include trunk and branches in a secondary sense. In each instance the
individual's intentions determine which objective attributes are incorporated into the subjective comprehension.

Within this system what may be said by a term or expression is determined by its objective comprehension, but what actually is said is determined by the subjective comprehension. The subjective
comprehension constitutes the meaning of the term in any actual use.
The text or statement produced incorporates only the attributes intended by the speaker. This point is crucial. The meaning is absolutely determinate in each situation of use of a term. If this were not the

---

28 Bierberg, "Does Sacred Scripture?," p. 183.
  29 Coffey, *Science*, n.p., quoted in Bierberg, "Does Sacred Scripture?," p.
184.
  30 Coffey, *Science*, n.p., quoted in Bierberg, "Does Sacred Scripture?," p.
184.

case, all statements would be wildly ambiguous, every term in every sentence embodying all the attributes conceivable of the object to which it refers. "Subjective comprehension" is the principle of determinacy which allows a statement to express a single, fixed meaning. It allows no exceptions. Precisely what the author intended to say and only what the author intended to say is included in the text.

Bierberg's insistence on the determinacy of the subjective comprehension poses two problems for the *sensus plenior*. We have already seen one. If there were additional *sensus plenior* meaning in the text, it could be there only by by-passing the subjective intentions of the human author. Otherwise the additional meaning would be included in the author's intentions and would constitute the literal sense. But if the *sensus plenior* by-passes the human author, it is not the product of a process of inspiration and, paradoxically, the *sensus plenior* would not be inspired.

The second problem is new. Assuming that the *sensus plenior* somehow got into the text, if it were not part of the author's subjective intentions, it would constitute a formally distinct concept from that intended by the author. The logic is simple. The author's intentions produce one determinate sense. The *sensus plenior* is not included in that intended sense, so it is distinct and different. The determinacy of textual meaning then turns against the *sensus plenior*. The same text cannot have two distinct meanings. When the human author determines the subjective comprehension of his terms, all other attributes are stripped away and not carried into the text on peril of ambiguity. Consequently, once the author has ordered the text, in effect, to mean one thing, it cannot simultaneously mean another. What advocates of the *sensus plenior* point to as meaning in the text is not meaning at all, but later interpetation covered by the classification "accommodation." This accommodation is itself inspired because it is undertaken by inspired authors. Recognizing the inspiration of accommodation protects the traditional authority and esteem of the New Testament use of the Old Testament. The essence of Bierberg's argument, however, is a very firm rejection of the *sensus plenior* as logically incompatible with the principle of the determinacy of the text. If meaning is a determinate thing, it is only one thing.

In response Brown distinguishes between instances in which the author was dimly aware of the *sensus plenior* and instances in which he was not. In the first case Brown perceived no problem. The author intended, though somewhat dimly, to include the *sensus plenior* within the subjective comprehension of his terms.[31]

To analyze this notion of dim awareness within the logical framework provided by Bierberg is only to draw more attention to its incomprehensibility. At best, dim intentions would transmit dim comprehension to the text so that any subsequent revelation would discover only that same dim form. Even the obscurity transmitted to the text would be determinate! Here we strike against the limits of our imagination. Other questions plague the notion of dim awareness. Is there a threshold of dimness below which the intentions are too weak to add meaning to the text? The further the notion is pushed, the more absurd it appears. Even the category of dim awareness will not pull the chestnuts from the fire.

In regard to instances in which the author was unaware of the *sensus plenior*, Brown is forced to acknowledge Bierberg's logical point.[32] Bierberg's argument is simply a consistent application of the Thomistic logic Brown accepts no less than he. Brown does not attempt, therefore, to refute Bierberg but once again transfers the issue to what was in God's mind. The *a posteriori* observation that there is additional meaning observable in the text is Brown's starting point. If that meaning was accommodation, as Bierberg classified it, "this would mean it was not intended by God."[33] Brown rejects this suggestion because the New Testament authors and Church Fathers do not indicate that they are accommodating the text but that they are referring to its actual meaning. The meaning seems to reside in the Old Testament, and the New Testament authors and Fathers simply witness to it.

In returning to the *a posteriori* observation of additional meaning, Brown advances his strongest counterargument against logical objections. But it forces an unwelcome choice. The *sensus plenior* and the Thomistic logic are not compatible with one another. Either the observation of additional meaning is somehow faulty or Bierberg's logic is flawed. The incompatibility demands a decision. Bierberg faces the issue squarely and decides for the Thomistic system. In his dissertation Brown sidesteps, never refuting Bierberg nor rejecting the Thomistic

31 Brown, *Sensus Plenior of Sacred Scripture*, p. 127.
32 Ibid., p. 128.
33 Ibid.

logic. Brown leaves his observations of meaning in tension with the system supposed to explain their possibility. This is not an altogether satisfactory course.

One reason Brown can duck Bierberg's objection is that, although Brown has no direct answer to Bierberg's highly technical logical argument, he does feel he can allay the concern behind the objection. Bierberg is concerned to maintain the determinacy of the meaning of the text. To preserve determinacy Bierberg insists that the text can have one and only one meaning, the meaning intended by the author. To admit any principle which suggests that more than one meaning can reside in the text at once opens the floodgates to ambiguity and the sort of anarchy in interpretation which can destroy the essential authority of the scriptural text. Bierberg wants to confront the danger head on and place a firm block to its advance, an absolute principle of determinacy.

Brown is no more interested in uncontrolled interpretation or the idea of multiple meanings in the text than Bierberg. Although forced to admit that any *sensus plenior* would be a concept formally distinct from the literal sense, Brown does not accept the implication that this spells interpretive chaos. The *sensus plenior* must be homogeneous with the literal sense. Homogeneity provides a criterion by which to exclude arbitrary interpretation. The *sensus plenior* differs formally from the literal sense, but it is placed under the control of the literal sense and made subordinate to the determinacy of the text's literal meaning.

Homogeneity is a critical concept in addressing Bierberg's concerns, but homogeneity is itself a very difficult notion to grasp. It must be repeated that nothing in the basic definition of the *sensus plenior* requires it. God could intend a completely nonhomogeneous sense to be the *sensus plenior*. The principle of homogeneity is likewise not derived *a posteriori* from the practice of the inspired authors who provide evidence of the *sensus plenior*. There are many instances of these authors' interpreting Scripture in a more than literal way which Brown would exclude from consideration as *sensus plenior* because they are nonhomogeneous with the literal sense. The category precedes the correct classification of texts.

Even if homogeneity found a clear justification in the texts, it would still be very difficult to give a firm idea of its nature or find clear criteria for its application. Examining several examples used by Brown will illustrate the problems. The christological reading of Isaiah 7:14 constitutes the closest to unanimous candidate for the *sensus plenior*. In this well-known passage the original Hebrew contains the word *'almâ* which, it is now generally agreed, means "young woman" without regard to her virginity or even marital status. The Greek translators of Isaiah 7:14 settled on the word *parthenos* to translate the Hebrew. *Parthenos*, meaning specifically "virgin," is more narrow than *'almâ*. Brown holds that the concept "virgin" in the Greek translation is a homogeneous development from "young woman" in the Hebrew.[34] No definitive criteria of homogenity are given in this case, but the idea seems to be that "young woman" and "virgin" share essential attributes and so are homogeneous. The historical development from the earlier sense of "young woman" to the later sense of "virgin" testifies to the homogeneous relationship.

The Mass for the Sunday after Easter provides a negative example.[35] Wisdom 18:14-15, "For while all things were in quiet silence and the night was in the midst of her course, thy almighty word leapt down from heaven from thy mighty throne" is applied to Christ. This is not a case of *sensus plenior* because in the Wisdom passage, the "almighty word" is the destroying angel of the Exodus; in the Mass it is Christ and there is no homogeneity between the two.

What is this homogeneity present in the first case but absent in the second? There seem to be two possible ways to define a homogeneous relationship, either qualitatively or quantitatively. To establish a qualitative relationship there would need to be a single essential attribute in both concepts which would allow one to say they are homogeneous. The task is to specify what characterizes an essential attribute in more than an *ad hoc* way. There must be criteria by which to recognize the attributes of sufficient importance to establish homogeneity. Unfortunately, there are no obvious stable criteria. How do we know, for instance, in the case of Isaiah 7:14 that the essential attribute is "young womanhood," in which case homogeneity is present, and not "virginity," in which case it is not?

In order to establish a quantitative relationship, there would need to be a number of shared attributes. The task then is to establish criteria

---

34 Raymond E. Brown, "Hermeneutics," in *The Jerome Biblical Commentary*, eds. Raymond E. Brown, Joseph P. Fitzmyer, and Roland O. Murphy (Englewood Cliffs: Prentice-Hall, 1968), p. 617.
35 Brown, *Sensus Plenior of Sacred Scripture*, p. 145.

to locate the line of demarcation at which homogeneity fades into non-homogeneity because of too few shared attributes. In the passage from Wisdom above, the homogeneous attributes are that Christ too is called the Word and sits at the throne of God. Why are these shared attributes not adequate to establish a homogeneous relationship between the Wisdom passage and Christ?

One would not want to insist that Wisdom 18:14-15 is christological or Isaiah 7:14 is not. The issue is not whether these christological connections are convincing or useful but whether the specific concept homogeneity provides criteria for deciding which pairs of passages possess it and which do not. The conclusion must be negative. At best homogeneity would involve a complex calculus in each case, balancing qualitative and quantitative factors in an equation with most values unknown. Homogeneity is simply too vague and undefined to provide hard criteria by which to place a control on more than literal exegesis.

Most critical scholars worried about excesses in exegesis would certainly register the weakness of homogeneity as a defense against fanciful interpretations. The failure of the category therefore has important practical implications for the *sensus plenior's* apologetic function as critically respectable more than literal exegesis. But the failure is also important for its theoretical implications, because it fits into the pattern of problems stemming from fixing meaning as a hard and fast "thing." Considering meaning as a thing encourages one to construe the relationship of the meaning of two passages as a comparison of the attributes two things hold in common. If, then, one wants to speak of a particular type of relationship, homogeneity, it appears necessary to define a specific pattern of relations between attributes which defines the term. No specific pattern — homogeneity *per se* — exists which can cover all cases. Consider even the simplest case. Are apples and oranges homogeneous concepts? That depends. In a fruit bowl, they probably are. But if we are attempting to put a friend back on the logical track and say, "You are mixing apples and oranges," they are absolutely nonhomogeneous. To provide an account of homogeneity by reference to attributes and fixed meanings which will cover both cases is beyond our powers. It is not that we cannot talk about two concepts or two passages being homogeneous and make sense. It is just that we cannot formulate a rule with fixed criteria governing homogeneity, and this is what the notion of fixed meaning in the text would lead us to expect. And it is what Brown's practical use of the concept to exclude fanciful interpretations demands.

It is this notion of fixed meaning, meaning as a thing, which lies at the heart of the *sensus plenior* — and at the heart of its problems. The critical moment in the existence of the fixed meaning is the moment of its creation, when meaning is given its determinate form and content by the intentions of its author. That critical act of intention takes place in the mind of the author, an obscure realm not open to critical scrutiny by outsiders. In the case of the *sensus plenior* the determinate intentions are in the still more inaccessible mind of God. Treating meaning as an entity of a peculiar sort, a mental entity, allows the possibility of a *sensus plenior* by locating the critical moment of production of meaning in a completely unsearchable region. Of course, this would seem like mere sleight of hand were it not for the fact that the human process of producing meaning is equally obscure, taking place likewise in the inaccessible regions of human consciousness. Because the critical creative process cannot be perceived in human minds, there is no expectation that it could be perceived in the mind of God. The analogy with human creative activity is enough to allow the supposition that God creates and fixes meaning in the same way, by this mysterious process of intending. The idea that God creates additional meaning on analogy with the human creation of meaning thus seems a plausible hypothesis and, because the process is located in the hidden realm of consciousness, there is no fear of positive disproof. The core of the theory seems well insulated against refutation.

The danger in locating meaning in God's mind is precisely that because any consciousness in general and God's in particular is so hidden, it is not possible to determine with any assurance what is there and what is going on there. The hiddenness of the mind is an open invitation to speculation. To counter the tendency toward speculation in the theory, Brown insists that one work *a posteriori*, from observations of meaning in the text and not from speculation about meaning in the mind of God. It is a palpable fact, Brown argues, that when the New Testament and the Old are read together, there is meaning in addition to the limited literal sense of the Old Testament alone. This observation of meaning is unassailable as an observation. Brown then argues that because one can perceive meaning, it must have been put there by someone. That "someone" was not directly the human author, so it must have been God. It can therefore be concluded that the additional meaning was in the mind of God.

This line of argument seems virtually foolproof. The end of the argument that concerns God's consciousness cannot be refuted because there is no evidence that would tell against it. The other end of the argument rests on an empirical observation of additional meaning. Both ends seem unassailable. In fact, if only God and the text were involved, the argument would be very neat. It is the introduction of the human author that makes matters messy. There is no role and, indeed, no room for the human author because the *sensus plenior* meaning has already been fixed before the human author enters the picture. God has taken over the position of the human author. But the human author cannot be so simply factored out of the process. The human author wrote the final text. This is beyond question. Some account must be given of the human author's participation in the *sensus plenior*. In trying to give that account, the whole theory unravels in the ways we have seen. The whole central step in the argument which involves the human role seems *ad hoc* and apologetic because it is not possible to join the idea of meaning already fixed by God with the human author's proper nature as a creator of meaning. The strict analogy of God as author with man as author comes back to haunt the theory by making the human author, the one certain point, superfluous.

The notion of meaning as a thing placed in the text even creates problems for the *a posteriori* observation of meaning. It is not a problem with the observation itself, but with the explanation of it. The idea that meaning is an entity in the text leads one to argue that any meaning seen in the text must have been in the text from its creation. The christological meaning of Isaiah 7:14 must have been in the text from the moment Isaiah wrote it. But if this were the case, why was it not seen by anyone earlier? Why was further revelation necessary at all? One is forced to assume that this meaning was somehow concealed in the text, objectively there but hidden. Such a hypothesis, viewed coldly, looks very improbable and consequently it turns back against the original observation of additional meaning. If one is forced by the theory to defend a hidden christological meaning in Isaiah's own time, it is easier to deny the observation of additional meaning. The notion of meaning as an entity finally undercuts the strongest support of the theory, the reader's direct experience of meaning beyond the critical literal sense.

In subtle ways, meaning as an entity also undercuts the apologetic function of the *sensus plenior* with regard to critical scholars. Catholic critical scholarship involves not just a commitment to reconstructing the intentions of the author, but also a commitment to a body of controlled, scientific methodologies directed to an objective reconstruction of an entity, the literal sense of the text. The *sensus plenior* does not offer a special body of controlled methods appropriate to its object nor does it appropriate critical methods. But if the *sensus plenior* is an objective thing, there should be objective methods to discover it. Either the recognized methods of regular critical scholarship or other methods especially suited to the peculiar nature of the *sensus plenior* should apply.[36]

No methodology has become associated with *sensus plenior* and, consequently, while many critical scholars were attracted to the theory of the *sensus plenior* at one time, they have gravitated away from its actual use in exegesis because there is no possibility of critical discussion of the *sensus plenior*. Brown at one point conceded that he made very little use of the *sensus plenior* in his exegesis and added that he had heard from students that the same was the case for Joseph Coppens.[37] Given the critical temperament of the time, the theory cannot maintain that the *sensus plenior* is an object without providing a methodology to discover it.

The theory of the *sensus plenior* substitutes for critical methodologies the testimony of inspired authors to the presence of additional meaning in certain texts. But even this appeal to inspiration cannot stand against critical inquiry. It invites the question how the inspired authors were themselves able to discover the additional meaning. It quickly becomes apparent that their discernment of extra meaning did not result from controlled, objective inquiry, the type ap-

---

36 Catholic critical theory is very positivistic and objectivistic, with great confidence in the ability of criticism to reconstruct its object. Dilthey has had little impact on Catholic criticism. The goal is always an objective reconstruction. This strong belief in the possibilities of criticism heightens the skepticism among Catholic critical scholars of all non-objective exegetical methods. For a brief criticism of Catholic positivism, see James Robinson, "Scripture and Theological Method: A Protestant Study in *Sensus Plenior*," *CBQ* 27 (1965), p. 20.

37 Brown, "Problems," p. 462.

propriate to discovering an object. Brown says that he "exposed" some of his best students to patristic exegesis and they uniformly found it unconvincing.[38] Could the Fathers actually have discovered the *sensus plenior*? The problem is that criticism has an exclusive franchise on methods to discover objects, so that so long as the *sensus plenior* is regarded as an object, critical standards will stand in judgment of all other means of discovering it, such as patristic exegesis. Criticism is imperialistic; it tends to exclude all meaning not derived by its principles. It has largely forced out the *sensus plenior*.

Conclusion

It is safe to say today that the *sensus plenior* is a dead letter for nearly all Catholic exegetes.[39] Theoretical weaknesses in the theory itself provide one explanation for its demise. The Thomistic theory of reified meaning which underlies the *sensus plenior* stresses the determinacy of meaning and the *sensus plenior* must run head on against that principle of determinacy. Practical considerations also contribute to the downfall of the *sensus plenior*. The theory was designed to be compatible with, even subordinate to, critical scholarship. Critical scholarship had a determinate object to reconstruct — the human author's intentions — and, therefore, so did the *sensus plenior*. But critical scholarship also had a methodology with which to reconstruct its object and the *sensus plenior* did not. Consequently, the *sensus plenior* could not stand on equal footing with critical scholarship and has been forced out.

Is anything left of the *sensus plenior*? The single part of the theory that withstands attack is also the most important, the straightforward, *a posteriori* observation of additional meaning when the Old Testament

---

38 Ibid., p. 463.

39 Interestingly, *sensus plenior* has recently attracted interest in conservative Protestant circles. The situation in conservative groups is very similar to the position of Catholic scholars sixty years ago when the *sensus plenior* was first developed. See William LaSor, "The *Sensus Plenior* and Biblical Interpretation," in *Scripture, Tradition, and Interpretation: Essays Presented to Everett F. Harrison*, ed. W. Ward Gasque (Grand Rapids: William B. Eerdmans, 1978).

and the New are read together. That is the single positive value. The only other value of the *sensus plenior* at this point in the hermeneutical discussion is negative. The development of the theory demonstrates conclusively, I believe, that the additional meaning that can be observed cannot be explained in a system that reifies meaning, that treats meaning as a mental entity. Entities are determinate and a simple principle of parsimony will not allow us to recognize more than one in a text. Further, the failure of the *sensus plenior* shows, again conclusively, that the meaning established when Old Testament and New are read together cannot be justified by principles derived from critical scholarship. Critical scholarship forces the additional meaning out of consideration.

To do justice to Raymond Brown and also to acknowledge my admiration for the seriousness of his work, I must say that Brown has seen the problems with the *sensus plenior* and developed his own thought in a consistent way to combat them. In "The *Sensus Plenior* in the Last Ten Years," his first return to the subject after his dissertation, Brown began to move away from the concentration of the theory on the author's consciousness and on the fixed, objective nature of the meaning produced by that consciousness. In "The Problems of the *Sensus Plenior*," two years later, Brown expressed skepticism about the Thomistic roots of the theory and began the sort of hermeneutical reflection necessary to break the linkage to the Thomistic theory of meaning and also the subordination of the *sensus plenior* to critical scholarship. Brown was guided in part by James Robinson's reflections on the *sensus plenior*, in which Robinson had seen points of contact between the theory of the *sensus plenior* and the hermeneutical theories of Heidegger and Gadamer. Brown had also written in the meantime on Bultmann and the post-Bultmannians and a whole new world of hermeneutics centered on language and the text opened up. The issue of the creation of meaning in a consciousness receded, replaced by a greater interest in the *a posteriori* given, the text's own meaning. In his latest hermeneutical work, Brown moves even further in the direction of an exclusive interest in textual meaning, speaking now of several meanings, the original historical meaning, a canonical meaning, and what the text means now. Significantly, the *sensus plenior* does not figure in these considerations but is left behind with the Thomistic system in which it is formulated. Brown's latest work thus points the way out of the limitations of the *sensus plenior*. There will be reason to return to it again in my conclusion.

Chapter 3

Luis Alonso-Schökel

In *Theory of Literature*, René Wellek and Austin Warren drew a basic distinction between two approaches to literary study. Extrinsic criticism explains phenomena in the text by reference to forces and influences external to the text itself, forces operative in the production of the text. The fundamental explanatory mode is causal. "Though the 'extrinsic' study may merely attempt to interpret literature in the light of its social context and its antecedents, in most cases it becomes a 'causal' explanation, professing to account for literature, to explain it, and finally to reduce it to its origins (the 'fallacy of origins')."[1] The text is firmly anchored by chains of causality in the familiar world studied by the disciplines of sociology, psychology, anthropology, and history, the world accessible to controlled, scientific study. Intrinsic criticism addresses the text as a self-contained system of strictly literary features. The predominant mode of explanation is structural and relational. Each literary feature takes its significance and meaning from the patterns of relations it establishes with other features of the work. Each work constitutes an autonomous world, comprehensible in itself.

The relationship between these two approaches to literature can scarcely be given positive definition. Because of the broad difference in mode of explanation, causal versus structural or relational, it is difficult to find either arguments or terminology suitable to both. One continually lapses into one of the modes, failing to do justice to the other. Wellek and Warren's discussion of the relationship is largely negative, warning of infringement or curtailment of one sort of criticism by the other. In particular they are most concerned to defend the

---

1 René Wellek and Austin Warren, *Theory of Literature*, 3rd ed. (New York: Harcourt, Brace and World, 1956), p. 73.

domain of intrinsic criticism against imperialist claims by extrinsic critics exclusively to represent proper critical method. The significance of a work, they hold, exceeds the sum of the forces that produced it:

> [I]t is clear that causal study can never dispose of problems of description, analysis, and evaluation of an object such as a work of literary art. Cause and effect are incommensurate: the concrete result of these extrinsic causes — the work of art — is always unpredictable.[2]

There is in this statement, if not specification of the relationship between extrinsic and intrinsic criticism, an indication at least of their priority and range. The incommensurate effect, the work of literary art, lies beyond the competency of causal explanations in an area appropriately considered by intrinsic methods. Extrinsic explanations are of relatively limited range and give way to intrinsic considerations.

Commitment to the extrinsic methods of criticism was virtually unanimous among Catholic critical scholars of the period immediately following the promulgation of *Divino Afflante Spiritu*. Biblical scholarship needed a firm scientific footing. New and powerful scientific methods and disciplines revealed hitherto unknown forces active in shaping the biblical books. Archaeology, new historical rigor, developments in anthropology, sociology, psychology, and philology brought an explosion in knowledge of the biblical world. Much of this information could be related causally to the biblical text, so that major progress in understanding the motives behind the text seemed continually to be made. Luis Alonso-Schökel was among the first to move away from this methodological consensus, adopting instead methods associated with intrinsic criticism. Alonso-Schökel began his career teaching secular literature, using methods of comparative stylistics developed by Leo Spitzer, Helmut Hatzfeld, and Damaso Alonzo which we would recognize as intrinsic criticism. It was natural for him to apply his experience and productive methods to biblical literature when he turned his attention to Scripture. The first result of the effort to apply intrinsic methods to biblical texts was Alonso-Schökel's remarkable dissertation, *Estudios de poética hebrea*. It is easy to recognize in this work the influence of Spitzer's *Stilstudien* in its close, meticulous attention to nuances of style.

---

2   Ibid.

The numerous studies of Hebrew stylistics which preceded Alonso-Schökel's dissertation for the most part were content to catalogue and label the various literary effects. Alonso-Schökel went decisively beyond these studies, considering the literary effects not simply esthetic ornaments and arabesques, but semantically productive elements in the meaning structure of the total work. This position at once accepts the major premise of the intrinsic approach—meaning is a function of the pattern of literary relations within a text—and gives new seriousness to the study of stylistic features—they are constitutive of meaning, the exegete's fundamental concern.

Alonso-Schökel's analysis has three stages. The first is descriptive, identifying and describing the literary phenomena. The second is interpretive, articulating the semantic value of the phenomena described. The third is inferential, drawing conclusions about the mentality of either the author or the nation on the basis of their choice of literary devices. Each stage raises important hermeneutical questions warranting individual consideration.

The first stage, the description of literary features, is not the heart of Alonso-Schökel's study, though it is precise and, in the case of phonic effects, exhaustive. The use of various phonic effects, particularly in Hebrew poetry, had been noted before and their simple description would appear noncontroversial, a matter of accurate description of what lay open in the text. Any sequence in the text meeting the definition of alliteration, for instance, qualifies as alliteration. But comparison of Alonso-Schökel's list of phonic devices with those of other scholars shows that the matter is not so straightforward. To return to the example of alliteration: Alonso-Schökel's list is far more extensive than that in the classic study by Immanuel Casanowicz, *Paronomasie in the Old Testament*. Casanowicz excluded from consideration all instances which, while meeting the formal definition of alliteration, result simply from the coincidence of the same morpheme in grammatically related forms within a stanza. The repetition of the morpheme *yi-* in recurrent *yiqtol* verb forms would not constitute alliteration for Casanowicz.[3] For Alonso-Schökel it would.

---

3 Immanuel Casanowicz, *Paronomasie in the Old Testament* (Boston: Norwood Press, 1894), pp. 27-28.

This narrow controversy immediately calls forth the question of how
it is to be settled. Clearly the matter cannot be settled at the descriptive level. There can be no dispute that two *yiqtol* verbs begin with the
same sound. The question is whether this repetition of sound is alliteration. As it stands, this question seems to involve hypotheses either
about what the author intended — he intended repeated *yiqtol* forms to
be taken as a significant phonic effect or he didn't — or about what a
hypothetical Hebrew-speaking audience heard — they heard an alliteration or they didn't. Casanowicz explicitly makes alliteration
depend on the author's intentions, hence all accidental or grammatically conditioned coincidences drop from consideration.[4] The author
could not intend them because he did not have the freedom to avoid
them. Alonso-Schökel seems to agree that intention decides the matter, differing only in taking a broader view of what the author could intend. The author was free to exploit the full resources of the language,
including stylistic effects built into the language.[5]

It should be clear that as long as the issue is construed as rival
hypotheses about the limits of intentionality, there is no meaningful
data that can be brought to bear on it. The situation is even more acute
than in normal arguments about intentionality in which external data
about the situation of utterance can bestow a certain probability on one
or another hypothesis about an author's intentions. In the case of
literary effects, there is no external evidence, only the undisputed
descriptive facts of the text itself, which accept either interpretation.
External data would only be available if we could consult either the
author or the original audience about the conventions that governed
such forms. By submitting sample texts to such an audience, we could
ascertain whether they recognized "accidental" alliterations as true alliterations — meaningful stylistic effects — just as we might ascertain
that modern readers of English poetry do or do not perceive one-syll-
able prepositions as alliterative. Either the original author or the
original audience could presumably settle the matter. But as a matter
of fact, neither is available nor is any other evidence which would establish the author's intentions. The result is that even the categoriza-

---

4 Ibid., p. 26.

5 Luis Alonso-Schökel, *Das Alte Testament als literarisches Kunstwerk*,
trans. Karlhermann Bergner (Cologne: J. P. Bachem, 1971), p. 2.

tion of Hebrew stylistic effects remains hypothetical to the extent that the categories are held to rely on reconstructions of the author's intentions. The problem is most serious as one moves to the margins of descriptive categories, often the most interesting but also most problematic cases. But the hypothetical character applies to all categorizations, even those which find the greatest degree of consensus among modern scholars.

The second stage, the heart of Alonso-Schökel's study and, in my view, its main contribution, is the semantic analysis of the literary features described. Considering stylistic features meaningful rather than ornamental is essential to a literary criticism that moves along internal lines within the text itself. An example will illustrate Alonso-Schökel's procedure.

Relatively early in his dissertation, Alonso-Schökel had noted as a descriptive fact a predominance of long a's and o's in Isaiah 6:3, the song of the seraphim.[6] In assigning semantic value to this literary feature, Alonso-Schökel says,

> The vowels a and o can symbolize greatness, majesty, fullness when they predominate, as for example in the song of the seraphim in 6:3. In 40:10, on the other hand, where there are various possessive o's of the third person, there is not such active effect. The divine promise in 57:19 provides us a similar effect: šalôm šalôm larahôk welaqqarôb.[7]

Something seems intuitively correct about Alonso-Schökel's suggested value for those long a's and o's, yet it is difficult to suppress a certain skepticism. Our mixed response requires further analysis. The plausibility of Alonso-Schökel's suggestion is enough to establish, if this is necessary, that stylistic features are semantically productive. This plausibility rests, I believe, on analogy with our response to the translated English text. qadôš qadôš qadôš comes into English as "Holy, holy, holy" (or into Spanish, Alonso-Schökel's native tongue, as "Santo, santo, santo"), obviously without the long a of the Hebrew, but certainly with the long, round o, reinforced (and this may be the effective factor in English) by the trochaic pattern of recitation which stresses and holds the long o. The stressed long o does contribute to a sense of

---

6 Ibid., pp. 46, 47.
7 Ibid., p. 75.

majesty when the English text is read aloud. It is not difficult to transfer this response to the Hebrew text.

But the unease we feel with Alonso-Schökel's suggestion also has a ready focus. What assurance have we that long a and long o symbolized majesty to ancient Israelites? The suggestion initially appears arbitrary and unsupported by more than the modern analogy. Alonso-Schökel does not claim that long a and long o, either together or singly, are morphemes signifying majesty. Such a claim, at least, would have the virtue of being easily tested by examining all Hebrew words containing the suggested morpheme. But Alonso-Schökel's claim is far more specific and, consequently, far more difficult to verify. Long a and o do not always signify majesty, but in the specific context of Isaiah 6:3, they do.

Two general arguments support the proposal. First, Alonso-Schökel follows the work of Friedrich Kainz, *Psychologie der Sprache*, who posits certain universal psychological impulses underlying all language. The universal quality of the psychological substrate strengthens the analogy between ancient usage and modern. Second, Kainz's theory makes literary phenomena the expression of a limited constellation of psychological impulses, increasing the probability that Alonso-Schökel connected the literary feature in the Hebrew text with the correct psychological impulse behind it.

This is not the place to review Kainz's theory in detail. Some form of analogy obviously exists between all language systems, otherwise translation would prove utterly impossible. Whether the analogy is to be located at the level of common psychology can be debated. And identifying semantic value with psychological impulse is unquestionably very narrow. But regardless of the merits or shortcomings of the psychological approach, it is clear that any theory of a universal substrate to language can only be of general relevance and limited application to the proper interpretation of individual stylistic features. This is so because of the principle, well established in linguistics, of the arbitrariness of the sign. The principle is not complicated. It denies that there is any natural connection between a sign — in this case a phonic device — and what it signifies. The relationship between sign and thing signified — in this case "majesty" — is purely conventional, the convention being in force only within the language system in which the sign functions. To take the boundary example of an onomatopoetic word: it might be supposed that the word "cuckoo" has a natural relation to the bird signified by it. The form of the word reflects the sound made by the bird. But the conventionality of even this most natural relationship is visible if we look at the German word for the same bird, *der Kuckuck*. Presumably German cuckoos sound like American cuckoos, but the convention adopted to represent the sound differs in the different language systems. Onomatopoeia is the most natural of relations between sign and signified; all others are still more conventional. Applied to this specific case, the principle means that, confronted with the same objective phenomena in the two languages, the long o, we may not assume that both signify the same thing. Or, stated from the perspective of Kainz's psychologistic theory, given a desire to express a common feeling, majesty, we may not assume that English and Hebrew would realize that impulse through the same sign, a series of long o's.

Alonso-Schökel further argues that the semantic value of stylistic features can be established by comparison with other meaningful elements of the text with which they are semantically congruent:

> It is very important to keep in view that the phonic value of a word forms an inseparable unity with the meaning of the word and the context. Therefore it is possible without committing a methodological error or running in a circulus vitiosus to take the sense of a text as a starting point. Conclusions may then be expanded outward from the textual context.[8]

There is surely something to these considerations. Only in the case of some gibberish and nonsense rhymes do phonic devices provide the key to the full meaning of the text. Normally meaning results from the complex interplay of stylistic features, the lexical meaning of the words used, structural relations between elements, and the situation in which the language is used. Phonic effects may indeed reinforce other more easily recognized features, working in complete congruence to produce a single effect. In the English form of Alonso-Schökel's example, this would seem to be the case. The long o's and trochaic repetition reinforce the lexical meaning of the words, "Holy, holy, holy."

But it is a mistake to think that all the elements of meaning must agree in this one fashion, one layered on top of the other to a single effect. This constitutes one pole of the range of possible relations, but the range extends through infinite variation in nuance to spectacular

---

8 Alonso-Schökel, *Das A. T. als literarisches Kunstwerk*, p. 17.

incongruity, even ironic antithesis. Some unquestionably perceptible phonic effects may convey nothing at all. Alonso-Schökel and Casanowicz, for instance, differed on whether alliterations formed of recurrent morphemes were meaningful in some sense, although neither would dispute that they were perceptible. One may begin, as Alonso-Schökel suggests, with the clearest elements of meaning. But relatively clear elements such as lexical meaning are no sure guide to the precise contribution of other stylistic elements. If the assumption of identity of effect were correct, all stylistic effects would be semantically redundant, mere ornaments to meaning conveyed by other factors. Alonso-Schökel properly denies the mere ornamental character of stylistic effects. This denial implies, I would argue, a broader range of semantic relations than simple identity of effect. It is perfectly true that the other semantically effective elements in a passage, such as lexical meaning and grammatical structure, have a determinate form which influences and restricts the pattern of meaningful relationships into which stylistic effects can enter. This is obvious, though it does no harm to mention it. But to imply that stylistic effects in Hebrew are restricted in function to reinforcing meaning produced by other elements in a passage is another matter. If this were the case it would constitute a feature unique to Hebrew literature since other literatures admit a much broader range of semantic function of stylistic effects. In any case, Alonso-Schökel would have to demonstrate that stylistic devices were conventionally restricted to this one narrow function; he may not assume it. Such a demonstration is beyond Alonso-Schökel's powers since there is no pertinent evidence available. Thus far we may agree with Alonso-Schökel's argument: that the semantically relevant elements of a text form a determinate pattern into which stylistic features must fit. But the meaning pattern of a passage is not complete until the stylistic features have added their contribution.

Alonso-Schökel's general proposals are insufficient individually or in combination with one another to establish the semantic values of stylistic features as they were understood in ancient Israel. All of his proposals require additional information, on the intentions of the author, on the response of the audience, or on the general conventions that governed the use of stylistic devices. This information is not available. As a consequence, it is not possible to establish with precision the meaning of a passage as it was understood in ancient times.

This conclusion must appear fatal to the central focus of Alonso-Schökel's program. In fact, it is at least debilitating to any perspective that views the meaning of the text as a static quantity, fixed in the text at the time of composition, an object to be reconstructed. The best this view can produce is some measure of probability that it has hit upon the original sense of the text, accompanied by richly warranted skepticism. Alonso-Schökel's formulation of the semantic value of stylistic devices suffers from this static conception. The formulation is untenable, but the initial insight that stylistic features contribute directly to the meaning of a passage is well grounded in our experience and stands on its own.

In the third stage Alonso-Schökel proceeds to inferences about the mentality of the author of a work or of the nation in which it was composed. For Alonso-Schökel, language, including its stylistic aspects, is a psychological phenomenon, a direct expression of the mind that produced it. Differences in the pattern of usage of stylistic devices from one author to another represent differences in mentality between the authors. And systematic differences in stylistics between language groups or national groups may be attributed to differences in mentality between the nations involved. This notion derives originally from the metaphysical linguistics of Wilhelm von Humboldt, although Alonso-Schökel takes it most directly from the work of Friedrich Kainz, mentioned earlier.

The psychological orientation of Alonso-Schökel's treatment of Hebrew stylistics is evident in his discussion of synonymy and antithesis, two categories familiar from Robert Lowth's classic study of poetic parallelism. In Lowth's work, these two categories and a third, synthetic, were descriptive classifications very closely tied to corresponding features of the Hebrew text. Alonso-Schökel acknowledges Lowth's work, but reorients the categories from descriptions of literary phenomena to psychological processes. The reorientation is accomplished by designating synonymy and antithesis subdivisions of a larger psychological category called by Kainz "articulation" (*Gliederung*). "Articulation" denotes the psycholinguistic process which transforms an individual's raw experience into meaningful language. Experience itself is an inchoate continuum of impressions, neither meaningful nor communicable in itself. Articulation converts experience into language, in which form it is both comprehensible to the individual and communicable to another:

> The innermost articulation takes place in the region of the intellect and structures the whole of our psychological experience. This innermost articulation is the root of all language.[9]

In this psychological system, synonymy and antithesis constitute distinct stylistic means by which the undifferentiated continuum of experience receives determinate linguistic form.

It is important to notice which of the two means is employed, since the characteristic patterns of meaning into which they organize experience differ regularly. Following E. Norden in *Die Antike Kunstprosa*, Alonso-Schökel argues that by its nature antithesis is analytic. That is, it renders the prelinguistic continuum by drawing distinctions among the elements within it, using contrast to specify the complex relationships that comprise the whole. Synonymy, on the other hand, is comprehensive; it renders the continuum as a totality by providing encompassing terms.

This discussion provides only broad theoretical generalizations about the semantic value of antithesis and synonymy at this stage. But Alonso-Schökel carries it considerably further. Comparative study showed to Alonso-Schökel's satisfaction that antithesis predominates in Western literature while synonymy is the dominant mode of articulation in Hebrew literature.[10] It is a straightforward step to convert this comparative observation into conclusions about Hebrew mentality in contrast to Western. The warrant for those conclusions is the assumption that the structure of a language, as distinct from what is expressed using the language, is a manifestation of the collective mentality of the group using the language. Alonso-Schökel's specific conclusions read,

> In Hebrew literature synonymy or repetition predominates, in western literature antithesis or contraposition. This can be traced to the tendency among the Hebrews toward "totality," "integrity." They perceive a totality and articulate it with words in a simple sentence. Then they turn once again to the same totality and articulate it in another similar or equivalent sentence. They

---

9 Ibid., p. 207.
10 Alonso-Schökel provides his own study of Hebrew literature and relies on Norden for his characterization of Western literature.

perceive and formulate the totality as a datum and not as a problem. Europeans do not seek totality, but are compelled to differentiate, to make precise, to analyze, and to develop nuances. In the process the facts become a problem.[11]

The first part of Alonso-Schökel's argument, establishing that synonymy signifies totality while antithesis differentiates, whether successful or not, corresponds to the semantic analysis of literary effects discussed earlier, although on a much broader scale. One would want to review the evidence very carefully, but it is at least conceivable that synonymy and antithesis are the stylistic equivalents of morphemes. If confirmed, these fixed values for common stylistic devices would be highly significant interpretively. The validity of these determinations is an issue in itself, but wholly aside from it, the further step of drawing inferences about Hebrew mentality seems extraneous and largely unconnected with the interpretive task. Such conclusions can only draw on the results of assured interpretation. The suggestion that synonymy signifies totality, if it is valid, rests on the correct interpretation of every passage in which it appears. The addition of "mentality" to the analysis adds nothing interpretively. Its primary function seems to be to connect the textual feature to an independent reality in the outside world.

The concern for Hebrew mentality Alonso-Schökel exhibits has a long history in biblical studies, a line originating with Herder and represented in the period in which Alonso-Schökel was writing by the Biblical Theology Movement. Within this movement the closest parallels to Alonso-Schökel's arguments were the widely influential studies of Johannes Pedersen and Thorleif Boman. Both Pedersen and Boman attempted to draw conclusions about differences between Semitic mentality and Western, "Greek," mentality from differences in the grammatical structure of the languages. As we have seen, Alonso-Schökel draws parallel conclusions from the stylistic structure of the language.

Since both Boman and Alonso-Schökel describe the same mentality, it is reasonable to expect their conclusions to agree. But the disquieting fact is they do not. Oddly enough, they arrive at exactly opposite conclusions. Boman holds that the characteristic process of Hebrew thought is differentiation, the analytic drawing of distinctions. As we

11 Alonso-Schökel, *Das A. T. als literarisches Kunstwerk*, p. 303.

have seen, Alonso-Schökel finds the characteristic process to be the description of a totality; distinctions are alien to Hebrew thought. These conclusions are irreconcilable and one is led to draw one's own conclusion that the fundamental assumptions are faulty.

In fact, Boman's work passed under a cloud from which it has not emerged with the appearance of James Barr's *The Semantics of Biblical Language*. Barr's work, however, does not vindicate Alonso-Schökel's conclusions. Barr's criticisms apply equally well to Alonso-Schökel.[12] Barr required — and today it seems completely obvious — that assertions about Hebrew mentality be based not on isolated features of the language but on a consideration of the total language system.[13] What is not expressed in the language in one way may be realized in another. The alleged impoverishment of Hebrew adjectives is made good by the construct chain, in which nouns are used adjectivally.[14] In the case of stylistics the "totality" conveyed by synonymy is balanced by fine distinctions drawn using repeated circumstantial clauses, as in casuistic law. Very fine distinctions can be made in specifying the application of the legal principle. Obviously, Hebrew minds had no difficulty drawing precise distinctions when the situation demanded.

The remainder of Barr's criticisms are well known and their validity widely accepted. There is no need to apply them point by point to Alonso-Schökel's dissertation. The pall Barr cast over the effort to correlate linguistic structure with Hebrew mentality equally covers the effort to correlate stylistic structure with a distinctive mentality. Barr attacked specific proposals, but the force of his argument was so great and applied so broadly that it effectively undercut the plausibility of the whole notion of a direct correlation between structural features of a language and an underlying mentality. Most immediately the portions

---

12 Incredibly, Alonso-Schökel had read Barr and found the detailed criticism of Pedersen, Boman, Gerleman, and *Das Theologisches Wörterbuch des Neuen Testaments* justified. But he rejected without argument the general conclusion the detailed criticism required, that a straightforward relationship between mentality and the structure of the language cannot be demonstrated.

13 James Barr, *The Semantics of Biblical Language* (London: Oxford University Press, 1961), p. 24.

14 Ibid., p. 29.

of Alonso-Schökel's dissertation concerned with Hebrew mentality lose credibility. But the failure to establish a convincing correlation between language structure and mentality has wider implications. The tendency, represented strongly in Alonso-Schökel's work, to consider language and literature as psychological phenomena and to use psychological categories to describe them appears misguided and inappropriate. Correlations of the sort that would make the psychological categories productive cannot be carried through.

Alonso-Schökel's psychological orientation is also apparent in his attribution of the meaning he discovers in the stylistic devices to the intention of the author. Referring meaning to the author's intentions never received the explicit discussion given Hebrew mentality. That the meaning produced by the stylistic effects corresponds to the author's intentions is a tacit assumption, expressed by phrasing statements of the meaning of the stylistic features as "what the author meant" rather than "what the text says." Further, there is the assumption that controversies such as the one with Casanowicz's work are actually disputes over what the author intended. The assumption involved here—that the meaning of the text is equivalent to the author's intention—is common in literary criticism and is largely consistent with the extrinsic approach to literature. The extrinsic approach focuses on the causes of the literature and the most immediate cause, it is held, is the author's intention. However, introducing intention into intrinsic criticism of the sort Alonso-Schökel practices raises serious issues.

The issues are complex but they can be illustrated by contrasting the way intentionality functions in extrinsic criticism with the way it functions in intrinsic criticism. If in an extrinsic interpretation one is confronted by a passage whose meaning is uncertain, proper method demands research on the circumstances under which the text was written. The assumption is that the author was influenced in what he wrote by those circumstances. By assembling information on all the pertinent forces that affected the author or circumstances to which the text was a response, the intentions of the author in producing just this text can be established with some probability. The author's intentions, the proximate cause of the passage, are then held to determine the meaning of the text.

There are practical and theoretical difficulties with this procedure, but at least intentions play an integral and comprehensible part in it. The case is otherwise with intrinsic criticism. In intrinsic criticism the meaning of the passage is a function of the pattern of relations among the literary elements of the text. Intentions do not play an immediate part. Establishing the meaning of a passage is a matter of recognizing the patterns and relations within the text and applying the appropriate conventions which govern them. If, then, one wants to speak of the author's intentions, it involves a second step. With the meaning of the text already known, one assumes that the author intended precisely this meaning. The purely formal character of this second step is readily apparent; one moves from known effect, the meaning of the text, to hypothetical cause, the intentions of the author. Nothing is added interpretively to the meaning by referring to the author's intentions because the meaning must be known before the connection can be made.

This procedure may be faulted. There is no independent evidence analogous to the evidence cited by extrinsic critics which would support the supposition that the meaning we derive from a passage is identical with the meaning understood by its author. Understanding the meaning of a passage involves both recognizing all the meaningful patterns existing among elements of the text and controlling the conventions which govern their interpretation. When we address an ancient text we cannot be certain that we perceive all the patterns the original author considered meaningful, that we do not consider meaningful patterns the author did not, or that we employ the same conventions in interpreting the patterns we do share. Alonso-Schökel assumes that literature functions something like face-to-face communication, in which it is a fair assumption that the hearer and the speaker share the same conventions. If an error is made, the wrong convention applied, the speaker can correct the misunderstanding. In such direct communication it makes sense to speak of the hearer's understanding what the speaker intended. But the situation is quite different in the case of literature, particularly ancient literature, and no assumption of identity between what we understand and what the author intended can be made without additional evidence. But, in the case of intrinsic criticism as opposed to extrinsic, it is not clear what would count as additional evidence. Only information concerning the conventions governing literary devices in ancient Israel would be pertinent. Failing explicit contemporary description of the conventions or, obviously, someone directly conversant with them, the necessary information is not at hand. The assumption that what we understand in a literary device is what the author intended remains no more than that, an assumption.

Equally a matter of concern is the purely formal nature of the reference to the author's intentions. It adds nothing substantive to the interpretation of the text because, unlike intentions in extrinsic criticism, it adds no new information. Still further, intentional arguments can add nothing to intrinsic analysis because intentionality constitutes a causal hypothesis and causal hypotheses are irrelevant to intrinsic interpretation. Combining causal explanations of literary phenomena with explanations based on patterns of relationship between the phenomena can only lead to confusion about how the two types of explanation fit together.

If the reference to intentions adds nothing to an intrinsic interpretation and is potentially confusing, the question arises, why refer to them at all? What is at stake in this secondary move to the author's intentions? The answer never appears clearly in Alonso-Schökel's dissertation, primarily because his major interest in that work is describing the semantic value of individual effects. The answer only emerges as Alonso-Schökel turns his attention to broader theological issues and attempts to make a literary model productive in dealing with such traditional issues pertaining to Scripture as revelation, inspiration, the truth and authority of Scripture, and its proper use in the life of the church and in the liturgy. Throughout his discussion of these issues, which will be surveyed in the next section, Alonso-Schökel draws on two aspects of literature. First is the autonomy of the meaning of the text. The meaning of the text resides in the text itself, where it is immediately accessible to the reader. This is the working assumption made in intrinsic criticism and correlates with the methods used by that approach to literature. The second aspect of literature is its ability to point beyond itself into the world outside. Alonso-Schökel gives this principle a particular turn which must be carefully noted. His focus is not on the directly referential potential of literature. Rather, he traces literature's relationship to the world back through the genetic process by which it was produced. The introduction of the author's intentions and of Hebrew mentality already figured as examples of this means of connecting the literary text with some external reality. In fact, Alonso-Schökel's recurrent references to the author and the strongly psychological linguistic categories he used, both of which seem extraneous to his dissertation's central concern with intrinsic meaning, are best explained as efforts to connect the text with independent reality. The author represents the crucial link between the text and the world outside it. And the causal categories of extrinsic criticism provide the most suitable means to describe the connection.

Maintaining both principles and consequently both modes of criticism simultaneously is essential for Alonso-Schökel. By combining them in different ways or even playing one against the other, he is able to construct a broadly literary model which at once seeks to maintain fundamental teachings about revelation, inspiration, and the authority of Scripture, yet to take account of the changed understanding of the Bible current in the critical age. There is a reciprocal relationship between his literary theory and the traditional doctrines. On the one side, Alonso-Schökel redefines the traditional doctrines in concepts and terms drawn from literary theory. On the other, those fundamental aspects of traditional teaching which must be maintained shape the contours of his literary theory. The following sections analyze this reciprocal relationship and its consequences, beginning with Alonso-Schökel's treatment of revelation.

In the first chapter of *The Inspired Word*, Alonso-Schökel considers three media of revelation: through creation, through history, and through the word. The three are distinct, but Alonso-Schökel succeeds in unifying them by considering each a linguistic phenomenon. Creation can be considered language because it is "a well-ordered system of things" which "contains a differentiated yet ordered body of reality," a description reminiscent of Kainz's psycholinguistic category, "articulation."[15] Creation is like a language in which every created thing is a word. Creation may also be considered language because it is a manifestation of God. "Everything that God works outside Himself makes Him known and is a sort of language."[16]

It is important to notice the points of analogy between creation and language. Creation, like language, is a system, differentiated yet ordered. For Alonso-Schökel that order is the result of a psychological process, so that the order found in creation is attributable to a conscious act, the creative action of God. Second, language is an external manifestation of a person's being. This notion, too, is taken directly from Kainz's psychology, though there is a long tradition behind Kainz. The order of creation, then, is a language by which God communicates

15 Luis Alonso-Schökel, *The Inspired Word*, trans. Francis Martin (New York: Herder and Herder, 1972), pp. 32-33.
16 Ibid., p. 33.

his own being to the world. Creation, as language, converts God's inner experience into communicable form. This is a further hint at Alonso-Schökel's basic conception of language and, derivatively, of literature as a communicative medium through which that which is internal to one individual is communicated to another.

Although creation is a sort of language, it is only revelation "in a broad sense."[17] Creation, although analogous to language, is not formally language, and Alonso-Schökel maintains that only language — human language — is fully intelligible in itself and thus capable of being considered revelation.

Historical events likewise constitute an organized system analogous to language. Like the silent screen, the ordered set of images constituted by historical events communicates its message to those who experience the events. For ancient Israel, then, God's actions in its history represented a sort of language which revealed God to them. But the events of Israel's history — that original language — are no longer accessible to us.

> In the Old Testament, we find persons, events, and words, both of God and of men. We meet real human persons and God as a Person, we come to know real human events and see God as their protagonist, we hear real human words and we hear the Word of God echoing throughout all history. All of these come to us as language, in the strict ontological sense of the term. For the events do not happen again, nor do men live again to speak and reenact their original existence. These men and their actions have passed, and they reach us only as language.[18]

These last sentences contain an obvious truth. Events occur only once. We cannot return to them. Consequently, although historical events themselves constituted a language for Israel, they do not for us. This form of analogy between history and language, though appropriate for Israel, is not for us.

Rather, the analogy changes somewhat. Events do not recur. They cease to exist the moment they have passed. Yet, in some sense, the events are preserved by being transformed into language. The fact that events become history only through this necessary transformation into language provides a renewed warrant for treating history as a species

---

17 Ibid., p. 33.
18 Ibid., p. 124.

of literature. The analogy is much more strict and direct: history necessarily comes to us as language.

This form of the identification of history with literature is expanded
by consideration of the subjectivity of historical accounts. The quotation cited above might seem to indicate a conception of the historical
account as a direct linguistic correlate of the events it records, the only
difference being in ontological status. Existence in the real world is
transformed into existence in a literary work. But this is not the case.
At least since Dilthey there has been recognition of an irreducibly subjective element in history. The historian necessarily selects data and ar-
ranges its presentation in a manner determined partly by academic
interests, by the interests of the age, social class, nation, and so on.
Selection and arrangement are an inevitable and essential part of history. Unanalyzed data is not history. It is only the raw stuff of history
which the historian selects and presents in a meaningful way.

Alonso-Schökel connects the subjective element in history with
literature in a characteristically psychological way. Both the production of language and the subjective element in history rest on essentially the same psychological process. Articulation is the process of
selecting and ordering elements by which structure and therefore
meaning is imposed on an undifferentiated field of experience. History
involves precisely this process. The historian's mind converts the
universe of available data into an orderly, structured account. In effect
it transforms the chaotic historical experience represented in the raw
data into meaningful language.[19] The production of historical accounts
is thus fundamentally a linguistic process and the result of the process
is a literary entity, a piece of literature. History and literature are
unified by the common psychological process taking place in the
author's mind.

The result of the introduction of psychological theory into the
analysis of history is a reorientation of focus away from historical
events, which recede into the background as little more than raw stuff,
toward the productive activity of the author/historian's mind, or, more
properly, the direct result of that activity, the meaning imposed on the
data. History becomes in its essence interpretation, and it is properly

---

19 Ibid., p. 249.

the interpretation and not the events themselves which are of interest to us.

The Bible is history in precisely this sense. The biblical authors' "selection and arrangement of events convey in their telling their true interpretation.... Events become the narrated word, and thus receive their authentic interpretation through this word which raises them to the level of formal revelation."[20] But being classed as interpretation does not entail a reduction in historical value or authority for the Bible, since *all* history is interpretation.

The identification of history with interpretation and literature greatly expands the range of forms that a historical account can assume. History need not be restricted to the simple chronological recounting of events. "Of course, the sacred author maintains his right to use other facets of language in order to interpret events: speeches placed in the mouth of principal actors, introductions to his stories, reflections on them, and the rest."[21] Virtually any form of language can be history, so long as it expresses the author's interpretation of historical experience.

The advantages of this literary definition of history when applied to the Old Testament are obvious. First, the whole question of the historicity of individual events is relegated to the background as the emphasis switches to meaning and interpretation. It is possible to talk about the historical character of the Bible without bogging down in the defense of every detail. Details are simply the literary way the author chose to express his historical interpretation. They are "other facets of language."

Second, historical revelation is identified with the biblical text. The events themselves are gone and, though they were in a sense revelation for Israel, they are not even potentially revelation for us. Revelation for us is only the mediate historical interpretation contained in Scripture. This principle avoids any sort of historical reconstructionism which would use nonbiblical sources to reconstruct Israel's history, then equate that history with divine revelation, displacing Scripture.

A full critique of this treatment of history must wait until after discussion of the third medium of revelation, the word. At that point the

---

20 Ibid., p. 37.
21 Ibid.

whole theory of revelation can be analyzed as it applies to specific texts. But even at this preliminary stage it is important to register unease at the extreme to which Alonso-Schökel drives the subjectivity of history. History is the result of a psychological process in the mind of the historian. In what way does it differ from purely imaginative, unabashedly subjective production from the same mind? The difference is that the historian's mental processes operate on an objective base provided by historical events; they select and order phenomena independent of the historian himself. This would seem to be an adequate check against complete subjectivity without denying the irreducibly subjective element in historiography. The historian's audience is able to compare the historical account offered by the historian with the data on which it is based in order to judge its adequacy as an explanation, to correct obvious biases and oversights, and so on.

But by stressing the nonrecurrence of events and their resultant inaccessibility to us, Alonso-Schökel radically reduces the objective base of history. In theory the historical text is bound to events — the text points beyond itself — but in practice we cannot push below the stratum of the author's interpretation — the text is autonomous. Alonso-Schökel invites our attention, then, to the level of the author's interpretation, the level which constitutes the meaning of the text. The objective base of the text is allowed to recede into a purely formal relationship with the author.

The difficulties to which this subjectivism can lead are signalled in Alonso-Schökel's short note about "other facets of language." Among the "other facets" allowed the author is the right to place speeches in the mouths of major figures, a right the deuteronomistic historian frequently employed. But in historical study, speeches are usually considered the data that the historian is called upon to interpret, not the interpretation itself. Category distinctions carefully maintained in historiography between data and interpretation blur. This blurring amounts to more than localized confusion over whether one is dealing with data or interpretation. It calls into question the appropriateness of designating biblical narrative as history, because history relies precisely on a clear distinction between the interpretation and what is being interpreted. It must be said that it is far easier for Alonso-Schökel to apply subjective literary categories to the narratives of the Old Testament than it is to show in what sense they deserve to be considered history.

The third medium of revelation is the word. By "the word" Alonso-Schökel means in a narrow sense all the nonhistorical parts of the Bible, the parts that originate in an author's imagination rather than concrete events. This includes most of the prophetic literature, Psalms, Proverbs, and, in the New Testament, the letters. But "the word" also extends to the commentaries on historical events which constitute "the other facets of language." Although these commentaries and the historical narrative proper are related to events, they are still strictly literature and therefore "the word"; they are both history and the word at once. History and the word blend together.

The common principle uniting history and literature is the origin of language in a distinct process in the author's mind. Alonso-Schökel expands on this process in his discussion of the word. The word originates in an event in the private inner life of an individual. Before any use of language there is a protracted moment of raw experience of some sort, either emotional or intellectual. That moment passes. "Then we are free from the rush of the waters and we retreat some quiet distance, to confront ourselves reflectively with our new experience."[22] Reflection bestows form and structure on the inchoate experience by transforming it into language. In Kainz's terminology the mind produces language by articulating raw experience. "Thus, our experience becomes language."[23]

The order bestowed by language is not an inherent feature of the raw experience but, in a sense, it is imposed on experience by the author's reflection. In the process the raw experience assumes a form which, for the first time, is intelligible to the one having it and communicable to others. The language produced, in contrast to the underlying experience, is meaningful.

The conversion of experience to meaningful form involves a change in ontological status. Language does not have the same reality as the experience itself. "Language...never has the subsistent quality of a human person,"[24] just as historical accounts do not have the same ontological status as the events behind them.

---

22 Ibid., p. 38.
23 Ibid.
24 Ibid., pp. 40-41.

Here, more clearly than before, are the roots of Alonso-Schökel's insistence on the two principles of language. The text is autonomous because it is not possible to delve below it directly to a substrate which is itself meaningful. The substrate is inchoate. Only the text has meaning. On the other hand, the experience behind the text is more real than the text itself. It has independent existence in the world while the existence of the text is clearly subordinate to and derivative of that reality, hence the importance of linking text to external reality with as firm a bond as possible.

When experience is converted to language it becomes communicable for the first time. The author is able to reveal profound experiences to others. "Language embodies the apex of human revelation."[25] The author's readers in turn are enabled to contact the author's inmost personal experience – at least in a mediate form. Language establishes a communicative circle by which one person – one is tempted to use the romantic term "spirit" – touches another. In a sense, every utterance is autobiographical. The part of the hearer or reader is to move through the language to contact the author. The part of the author is to convert experience into a form communicable to others.

When this communicative model of language is given a theological setting by considering God the author of Scripture, its importance is obvious. The text embodies the inner experience of God, converted to language; it is a manifestation of God's being. Christians are able to move through the normal communicative process to establish contact with God, although in a suitably mediate fashion. It is not possible to experience God's being as God experiences it, just as one is not able to relive the inner experiences of another person. But it is possible to duplicate within oneself the meaningful, ordered expression of that experience through the communicative function of language. This is precisely the role of Scripture, to communicate the ordered form of divine experience to believers.

Revelation as communication of being is the conceptual center of Alonso-Schökel's thought on revelation. Revelation is communication and communication is language. This central equation unfolds into the

---

25 Ibid., p. 41.

linguistic/literary analogy which organizes his treatment of revelation. The goal of this treatment is to show in what ways it is appropriate to think of revelation as communication.

Beyond this general goal is a desire to deal with issues of theology and hermeneutics, to use the communication model to resolve problems and affirm beliefs. Most pressing was the need to provide an account of the way in which history is revelation. As Alonso-Schökel remarked, the events of history today seem either the working out of mechanistic principles or a scandal.[26] The modern eye is ill disposed to see the events of history as manifestations of God's providence. Alonso-Schökel therefore interposes the biblical authors between us and events, replacing our historical interpretation with theirs. Their interpretations, it can be maintained, are authentically historical because, like all history, they are the result of a productive mind ordering and organizing historical experience into a meaningful account. But, unlike our secularized history, the biblical interpretations are also revelation, because they authentically represent God's activity, a manifestation of God's being.

The linguistic/literary analogy also allows Alonso-Schökel to maintain the unity of revelation. To some extent this is important because God is a unity and therefore the revelation of God should be of one character. Conceiving revelation as language allows a unified conception without completely obliterating distinctions in the media of revelation. There are three distinct media, all of which are language.

The unity of revelation is equally important when applied to Scripture, the concrete locus of revelation. The distinction between history and literature, which could provide a principle for the dissection of Scripture, is relegated to the level of the substrate on which the author works. The mental process which produces meaning is identical in both cases, resulting in the equivalence of historical and nonhistorical parts of the Bible at the level of meaning. The common process involved in producing history and the word resists the elevation of either category over the other. At the same time it allows their integration. History and literature share the same nature because they originate in the same mental process. It should be possible to move back and forth between

---

26 Ibid., p. 33.

historical and nonhistorical parts of the Bible without disruption. Again, the full integration of the Bible seems to be demanded by the unity of God's being. Revelation as communication protects the centrality and the integrity of Scripture by focusing on the message communicated. The importance of the message, the meaning produced, is emphasized in the theory by stressing that there is no unmediated access to the substratum underlying the mental activity of the author. All we have is the order made of that substratum in the linguistic act. Scripture is the record of the result of that linguistic act. There is no pushing behind it to historical events that are themselves revelatory. The traditional position of Scripture as the full and complete embodiment of revelation is maintained.

The breadth of Alonso-Schökel's treatment of revelation, its ability to take consistent positions on so many theologically and hermeneutically significant issues, is impressive. But the adequacy of the theories involved can only be judged when they are applied to literary texts or literary problems. Because the theories involve suggestions about how to read Scripture, they must ultimately be judged exegetically, by their effectiveness in explaining or opening up biblical passages. An article Alonso-Schökel wrote concerning Genesis 2-3 illustrates the application of the theories and serves as an example.[27]

For precision it must be said at the outset that Alonso-Schökel's treatment of Genesis 2-3 is not a full exegesis but rather addresses a specific problem. The encyclical *Humani Generis* of August 12, 1950 declared that original sin "...proceeds from a sin actually committed by an individual Adam and which through generation is passed on to all and is in everyone as his own."[28] Its position on the historicity of the Fall is clear enough in this statement but the encyclical goes on to recognize a problem:

---

27 Luis Alonso-Schökel, "Sapiential and Covenant Themes in Genesis 2-3," in *Studies in Ancient Israelite Wisdom*, ed. James Crenshaw (New York: Ktav Publishing House, 1976).

28 Pope Pius XII, *Humani Generis* in Megivern, *Bible Interpretation*, p. 368; also cf. D & S 3897.

[T]he first eleven chapters of Genesis, although properly speaking not con-
forming to the historical method used by the best Greek and Latin writers
or by competent authors of our time, do nevertheless pertain to history in a
true sense, which however must be further studied and determined by exegetes.[29]

Alonso-Schökel takes up the question of the way in which Genesis 2-3
pertains to history and immediately gives the question a literary turn.
"To determine further the specific type of history with which we are
dealing, we must use literary criticism."[30] The immediate issue is genre,
the type of history Genesis 1-11 represents. The question of historicity,
which is the heart of the issue for *Humani Generis*, is avoided or at least
postponed until the type of history can be determined.

Humani Generis excluded myth from consideration as a possible
genre and Alonso-Schökel quickly dispenses with recent arguments
connecting Genesis 2-3 to myth. To establish the actual genre, Alonso-Schökel directed attention to a number of motifs in the Fall story
which are also common in wisdom literature: the snake, rivers cir-
cumscribing the globe, and the interest in the classification and naming
of animals. His conclusion is that Genesis 2-3 is wisdom literature.[31]

With the genre established, the next step would seem to be to examine the way historical data is typically used in wisdom literature. This
would not lead far. It has often been remarked how little Israel's wisdom literature was aware of its historical traditions. In any case, Alonso-Schökel's interest in establishing the genre did not lie in specifying
the nature of the literature or its relation to historical writing, but in arriving at the figure of the author. Since the genre is wisdom, the author
was a sage of Israel.

At this point Alonso-Schökel turns his gaze from the text itself and
the relationship of what is said in it to historical events toward the
author and his relationship to events. This is a highly significant step.
Alonso-Schökel does not provide a warrant for this step in the article

29 Ibid.; also cf. D & S 3898.
30 Alonso-Schökel, "Sapiential Themes," p. 470.
31 The validity of Alonso-Schökel's argument is not our concern.
However, ironically, James Crenshaw's article on "Method in Determining
Wisdom Influence Upon 'Historical' Literature," which follows immediately
after Alonso-Schökel's article in the anthology cited above, contains criteria
which would invalidate Alonso-Schökel's arguments point by point.

on Genesis 2-3. It must be sought in his definition of history as the result of a mental act of the historian. The question raised by *Humani Generis* concerning the type of history Genesis 1-11 represents has been transformed into a question about the characteristic workings of the sage/historian's mind.

Just at this juncture the importance of identifying the author as a sage emerges. The sage, unlike modern historians or even the best Greek and Roman historians, does not proceed by sifting and weighing concrete data. Rather, the sage calmly contemplates the meaning of things. In the case of Genesis 2-3 Alonso-Schökel imagines the sage simultaneously contemplating the origin of all sin and the course of Israel's own salvation history, the repeated cycle of God's promise, Israel's rebellion, God's forgiveness and rehabilitation of Israel. Then, by a process of what Alonso-Schökel calls triangulation—this is the productive mental activity of the sage/historian—the sage follows the line of salvation history backward, arriving at its origin in the actual event of the Fall. Alonso-Schökel's own description of the process is worth citing at length:

> Let us now suppose a thinker who extends the horizon to all of humanity and repeats to himself the words: "For there is no man who does not sin" (1 Kings 8:46). In pondering this situation and in searching for an explanation, the natural thing is to apply the triangular ascent to the origin of all humanity. In this mental process he does not project a subsequent event back into the past, nor does he project back in allegory the experiences of all men. He really returns to the original event. If history describes the narrative of an event that really occurred, then the narrator is writing history, even though in his method of investigation and in his exposition he may not be writing the technical history of the nineteenth and twentieth centuries. He arrives by reflection illumined by the historical revelation of Israel at a fact—not in all its details or even in its precise pattern. To analyze and explain the original fact, the sacred writer is aided by his experience of the history of God's mercies and the sins of his people. He sees the original sin as a rebellion against a command of God who had taken the initiative in giving. And history does not end with total punishment. He knows by experience that the mercy of God is without end. In the narrative development the hagiographer gives us the true meaning of the original event, guaranteed by his inspiration.[32]

This formulation gives rise to misgivings which impugn the whole theory. First, crucial terms such as "fact" and "event" have slipped their

---

32 Alonso-Schökel, "Sapiential Themes," pp. 477-478.

moorings in the logic of historical discourse and are awash in an uncharted sea. In historical discourse, both terms have what may be called a referential logic. When a historian writes of a fact or an event, he implies direct correspondence between the written account and a state of affairs in the world outside the text. Still further, the logic of these terms' use in history demands that, at least in principle, there be some means of confirming the referential relationship. There must be corroborative evidence in order to speak meaningfully of a fact or event.

Alonso-Schökel systematically distorts this essential logic. It is meaningless to speak of a "fact" but "not in all its details or even its precise pattern." The logic of the use of "fact" in history demands correspondence in a rigorous and demonstrable sense. It is equally impossible to speak meaningfully of a historical event when all correspondences are beyond the reach of verification because they occur in the inaccessible reaches of the author's mind. Effectively, Alonso-Schökel has placed the author's consciousness in the direct relationship to events demanded of assertions of fact or descriptions. Direct referentiality and verifiability, both essential to historical logic, are denied. The logical status of this ersatz history is questionable. How are we to proceed with such a text? We cannot use this sort of history in the same way as normal historical writing because we cannot perform the operations on it that make history meaningful.

There is further misgiving because Alonso-Schökel's sage seems so little like a historian. The sage does not proceed by gathering evidence or by any other identifiably historical method. He works by a process of triangulation using as points in his triangle not concrete events but the universality of sin and the existence within Israel of a consciousness that its relationship to God traced a cyclical pattern. In what sense is the sage recognizable as a historian? In what sense can it be said that he arrived at a concrete event through his contemplation?

Most troubling, perhaps, is the appeal made to inspiration. It is motivated by a recognition that historical discourse requires verification as a part of its logic. Speculation is not history, nor are creations of the imagination. But in the case of the Fall story, independent corroboration is impossible. From whom would it come? To retain the form of historical discourse Alonso-Schökel must find a principle of verification to replace the empirical data that is lacking. Inspiration offers the authority required and can be introduced easily because Alonso-Schökel located the crucial historical relationship in the mind of the author, precisely the area in which inspiration works. The sage's mind can be secretly guided in its process of triangulation to arrive at a historical event. There is no way to prove this did not happen. Unfortunately, there is also no way to prove that it did.

The difficulty with this substitution is obvious. In the critical or even the incipient post-critical age virtually no one not preoccupied with apologetics will accept inspiration as equivalent to empirical verification.[33] To accept inspiration in place of empirical verification in historical discourse creates a wholly different logic for terms like "event" and "fact," effectively redefining them and changing their application. An event guaranteed by inspiration is an event *sub specie inspirationis*. The logical status of such an event might be explored profitably, but it cannot be considered the equivalent of an empirical event. It would not be possible, for instance, to insert a fact guaranteed by inspiration alone into a reconstruction of the reign of a Babylonian monarch. The paradox of Alonso-Schökel's line of argument is that in trying to maintain some sense of the historical character of biblical events, he has created a class of fact that cannot be integrated with all other historical facts.

The weakness apparent in Alonso-Schökel's treatment of Genesis 2-3 infects his discussion of revelation, in particular his effort to unify history and literature by tracing both to a single mental process. Particularly on the historical side, the psychological explanation simply will not serve. Its inadequacy lies in the areas of the relationship of interpretation to fact and the nature of historical referentiality. Alonso-Schökel holds that it is the author alone who is related directly to facts. The reader's relation is not with the facts themselves but with a piece of historical literature. Because this literature was produced in a subjective human mind, it necessarily constitutes an interpretation of events. This interpretation may nonetheless properly be designated

---

33 I do not believe Alonso-Schökel would accept it himself. He draws on inspiration to guarantee only the fact of the Fall, not the details of the biblical account. Why does inspiration not also guarantee the details? Because, it seems, there is empirical data which bears on their historicity in the form of identical details in other ancient Near Eastern creation stories. To extend inspiration's guarantee to the details would invite head-on confrontation. Inspiration can guarantee the facticity of the Fall only because there is no possible empirical data to challenge it.

history, as long as its author's mental processes operated on an experiential base of historical fact.

This conception falls short on a number of counts. In the first instance it is simply not the case that we do not have access to the facts asserted in the text. Alonso-Schökel mistakes an ontological point for an epistemological. Events do not recur. But to speak meaningfully of a fact or an event does not require that there be direct experience of it — history is not the report of direct experience — but only that there be grounds and evidence for what we claim to know about it. The reciprocal is that when we are confronted by an assertion of fact in a historical account, our initial operation is to check sources, weigh evidence supporting that fact, and so on in order to gain access to it epistemologically, although not ontologically. That sort of operation is no less open to the reader than the author and is an integral and necessary part of reading history.

Second, Alonso-Schökel fails to observe that history demands at once a clear distinction between facts and interpretation, and a structured logical relationship between the two based on the priority of facts. Interpretations must be an interpretation of something. The facts have priority. Before they can be interpreted (even simply by selection and arrangement) they must be established as facts by documentation, corroboration, their self-evident factual character, or some other method that meets current evidentiary standards.

Once established, the facts may be interpreted. But the interpretation is distinct from assertions of fact. We recognize the difference in the way we proceed. Facts are verified by consulting sources, but interpretation is weighed and judged by its comprehensiveness, by its consistency, by its ability to explain the facts it presents, by its compatibility with other known facts not adduced directly. Normally there is no danger of confusing fact with interpretation nor of misconstruing logical priority. If the facts cannot be verified, we do not entertain the interpretation. Alonso-Schökel asks us to ignore this normal procedure and accept the interpretation without questioning the facts.

To summarize, the problem with the highly psychological conception of revelation when applied to history is that it forces the creation of a widely variant logic of biblical history which, although it is in some ways analogous to the normal logic of historical assertions, still diverges at critical points, particularly in ignoring the requirement of verification. Given Alonso-Schökel's interest in maintaining the historical connections of the text, it is ironic that the creation of a peculiar logic of biblical history separates biblical history from all others. Any attempt to connect this biblical history with history whose assertions are verified by evidence must entail confusion.

The implications of the psychological orientation on the literary side are equally disturbing. The psychological preoccupation can lead to an independent interest in the author. The result of this interest in the author can be a trivializing of significant details of the text. In a sensitive intrinsic study of the Eglon and Ehud story, Alonso-Schökel notes the play made on Ehud's left-handedness.[34] A Benjaminite (literally "son of the right") is left-handed. In his left hand, the wrong hand, he carries Israel's tribute, a most unusual tribute, the sword of death, a very left-handed tribute. Alonso-Schökel caps his description: "As the narrator said the three words 'present,' 'hand,' and 'tribute,' he smiled."[35] Now this introduction of the author is harmless, no doubt, a way of calling attention to the humor and irony of the text. But it is trivial and reduces an important index of how to read the story to the fleeting pleasure of a long-dead and, at that, anonymous individual. The importance of this detail is the contribution it makes to the mood of the story, not its relation to the author and his mood.

More disturbing than the triviality of such remarks is the misinterpretation introduced by supplanting the meaning of the text itself with hypothetical reconstructions of the author's psychological or emotional states. As W. K. Wimsatt warns, "There is the danger of confusing personal with poetic studies, and there is the fault of writing the personal as if it were poetic."[36] A case in point is Alonso-Schökel's treatment of the opening chapters of the book of Hosea.[37] Once again it must be said that this discussion is not an exegesis *per se*, but it is an explication of the text in terms of the author's psychology, the approach Alonso-Schökel seems to favor, and a full exegesis would not diverge from it markedly. Alonso-Schökel's reconstruction of Hosea's emotions follows most modern treatments in inferring biographical details

---

34 Luis Alonso-Schökel, "Erzählkunst im Buche der Richter," *Bib* 42 (1961), p. 149.

35 Ibid.

36 W. K. Wimsatt, Jr., *The Verbal Icon: Studies in the Meaning of Poetry* (Lexington, KY: Noonday Press, 1954), p. 10.

37 Alonso-Schökel, *Inspired Word*, pp. 188-191.

from the biblical passage. Hosea married a woman whom he loved deeply, but she proved unfaithful. Her unfaithfulness was a source of anguish until, in a flash of intuition, Hosea realized that his experience was a metaphor for God's relation to faithless Israel. Hosea then transformed this intuition and the pain of his experience into the first three chapters of his book.

It is apparent how perfectly this treatment illustrates Alonso-Schökel's psychological theory. The underlying stratum is the unreflected pain of Hosea's marriage. The intuition is the psychological moment that transforms raw experience into linguistic form. The linguistic expression is the first three chapters of Hosea. The hermeneutic task, then, is to move through the text to understand the pain, and then, at the theological level, to touch God's feelings when faced with our faithlessness.

But for all its brilliance and ease of application, this reconstruction is not what the text says. In fact it runs directly counter to the plain sense of the passage. Hosea does not ponder his own dismal experience and find God's will in it. God's will confronts Hosea, "Go, take to yourself a wife of harlotry and have children of harlotry," and his bitter experience grows out of obeying the command. Tracing the passage to its genesis in Hosea's personal experience softens and distorts it. Ultimately it replaces the relatively plain sense of the text with a hypothesis rooted outside the text about an author unknown to us except as we meet him in the text.[38]

If the conflict between the meaning of the text and the psychological situation of its origin forces us to look more closely at Alonso-Schökel's procedure, we will be struck by the peculiarity of it. Alonso-Schökel seeks to infer Hosea's inner experience from the text of the first three chapters of his book. This should be unproblematic. According to the communication model the text is the objectified, communicable form of Hosea's experience. Now, using the model, it would

---

38 I do not mean to imply that the author's biography is immaterial, especially in passages such as Hosea 1-3, which are dominated by self-referential language. At issue here is not the important use of self-reference in biblical literature – the pain of fulfilling God's command is depicted autobiographically in Hosea – but the substitution of a biographical hypothesis about the causes of the text for the meaning of the text itself.

seem consistent, though largely uninformative, to argue that Hosea's experience corresponded to the plain sense of the text. If the argument were consistent, Alonso-Schökel's description of the psychological situation of the origin of the text would center on Hosea's experience of God's command, because that is what the text describes. Instead, the account presented centers on Hosea's domestic experience. This peculiar twist in the argument forces us either to reject Alonso-Schökel's reconstruction or to accept that Hosea did not accurately convey his experience — he meant to talk about his own experience but inadvertently fell into talking about God. The final alternative is that he did not mean to trace his understanding of God back to his own domestic woes. In this case, Alonso-Schökel's reconstruction of his psychological experience is misleading.

It is not clear what motivates the false steps in the argument. It may well be simply that the naturalistic psychological account is a closer analogy to our own experience than the supernatural account a direct inference from the narrative would require. But the motivation may be deeper. The consistent line of argument from the text to actual experience would require that God commanded Hosea to commit an unseemly act, namely, take a harlot as wife. This would lead to unacceptable inferences about God, especially in Alonso-Schökel's model. By making Hosea's unhappy experience precede his formulation of the command from God, the moral problem is avoided. God did not actually make such a command, Hosea just understood his own experience that way. This explanation solves the moral problem, but, to say it once again, it breaks the direct relationship between textual meaning and experience which is the basis of the whole system.

There is, I believe, no way out of this morass. Either the textual meaning is identical with the underlying experience, in which case one or the other is redundant, or the textual meaning is not identical with the underlying experience, in which case the experience is irrelevant at best, misleading at worst.

Examination of Alonso-Schökel's discussion of the important literary feature "tone" points to the same negative judgment on the psychological center of his communication theory. Alonso-Schökel's definition of tone is consistent. Tone is the concretized mood of the author at the moment of composition. "The attitude or 'tone' of soul on the part of the author determines the way in which the work is concretized as it receives its objective existence; in turn, the work determines the 'tone' which the sympathetic reader will derive from it."[39] The movement is familiar: subjective mood to objective text to resubjectified mood in a "sympathetic reader."

The problems emerge as soon as we begin to think about concrete examples. Alonso-Schökel provides several: "The author of the Book of Judith envisaged his protagonist in an 'heroic tone,' while the tone of gentle irony pervades the characterization of Jonah."[40] Alonso-Schökel's definition of tone suggests that the authors of Judith and Jonah had some "attitude of soul" or emotion corresponding to this heroism or irony as they wrote. But what would this be? Were they feeling heroic or ironic themselves? Would it destroy the effect in the text to find that they were coldly concentrating on the literary enterprise of creating a heroic or ironic effect? The point is that we do not normally suppose that an author was actually experiencing the emotions imparted to the text. When we do, we normally recognize that we are being very romantic about literature.

These passages exemplify the problems created on the literary side by the pronounced psychological orientation of Alonso-Schökel's model. First, the theory can give rise to discrepancies between the psychological state of the author of a text and the meaning of the text itself. This was the case with Hosea. The discrepancy forces a choice, either the psychological reconstruction or the plain meaning. Second, as "sympathetic readers," we must register our response that we simply do not refer overtly literary features of a text, such as its tone, to the psychology of the author of the text. Normally we make no inferences about factors outside the text from such literary effects, but interpret the effects strictly for their implications for the meaning of the text.

It was noted above that the incompatibility of the psychological reconstruction with the plain sense of the text forces a choice. Alonso-Schökel opts for the psychological reconstruction, perhaps, as I sug-

---

39 Alonso-Schökel, *Inspired Word*, p. 206.
40 Ibid.

gested, because the implications of the plain meaning when taken as a communication of God's being are very unwelcome in the case of Hosea. There are broader theological considerations as well. Alonso-Schökel would like to conceive of all Scripture as a communication from God, a linguistic manifestation of God's being. Consistently favoring a psychological interpretation of language, even with regard to the human author, makes the relationship of biblical language and divine being very direct. But Alonso-Schökel's choice of the psychological state of the author over the plain sense of the text seems wrong on several counts. First, it fails to recognize the practical priority of the meaning of a text. If one has a clear sense of the meaning, then one must cut the psychological reconstruction to fit the cloth provided by that meaning. In the case of Hosea, where the meaning is not particularly obscure, we may judge Alonso-Schökel's reconstruction either inadequate or wrong, because it fails to account for the meaning. The meaning is the standard of judgment of the psychological reconstruction and not the other way around.

The whole focus on the author's psychology is further imperiled by the difficulty and uncertainty of inference about the author's mentality. W. K. Wimsatt draws attention to what is no more than a verbal paradox when he notes that what is internal to a text is public and open while what is external – its author's mentality – is private and obscure.[41] The author's mentality is deducible only by inferences. Alonso-Schökel seeks to strengthen the inference by conceiving of biblical literature as communication. If I look you in the eye and say, "I am sad," you may fairly assume that I feel a sense of sadness which I am communicating to you. Communication tends to be direct and inferences about inner states generally warranted. But literature is different. One may not infer that every mystery writer is a murderer, either actually or in his secret heart of hearts. Inferences must be far less direct or suspended altogether. The block to direct inference in literary works lies in the uncertain reference of details. A main character in a novel may dine on Beef Wellington and Chateau Petrus because the author has a taste for it or because the story demands the character be depicted as a lover of luxury. But even in such a case the governing assumption of reading

---

41 Wimsatt, *Verbal Icon*, p. 10.

convention must be that the reference is internal to the literary work in the first instance and has its primary function there. It would be ridiculous to depict a hobo dining on such a meal, no matter what the author's personal preferences in food. In literature we cannot and do not draw direct inferences about the author on the basis of details of the story as Alonso-Schökel does in the case of Hosea. The communication model he adopts is simply too narrow to fit our experience of literature, including biblical literature.

From both the historical and the literary side, the placement of the author's psychological processes in the center as a unifying, organizing principle leads to very unsatisfactory results. The principle cannot unify history and literature without destroying the fundamental logic of one or the other. Nor does it preserve the two principles of the autonomy of the text and the external referentiality of the text, but places them at loggerheads.

Alonso-Schökel's psychological theory does fit well with traditional conceptions of inspiration. To make this connection is certainly a major aim of his psychological orientation. Alonso-Schökel shows by a survey of official Church pronouncements and the teachings of ancient fathers, medieval theologians, and modern scholars that inspiration has been viewed primarily as a psychological phenomenon. A significant minority position locates inspiration in the work itself but the dominant position focuses on the author. Alonso-Schökel's own psychological literary theory is designed to be consistent with the majority position and does not go beyond it except in its insistence that inspiration is limited to a linguistic process. The linguistic process is the process of articulation described earlier, which moves from raw experience through an intuition to the executive stage in which language actually appears. Inspiration does not apply to the first stage. Raw experience is prelinguistic and uninspired. But both the intuition, which first introduces order to experience, and the executive stage, which gives full and adequate linguistic expression to the intuition, are guided by inspiration.

The psychological theory of God acting directly on an author's mind developed when it was possible to think of a single author for each of the biblical books or even for whole complexes of books. Moses wrote the Pentateuch, David the Psalms, and each of the prophets the book bearing his name. Alonso-Schökel realized that critical scholarship, which found a far more complex compositional history behind the biblical books, raised problems for the traditional view. The standard view of authorship as a single creative act of genius no longer fit. A thousand authors, editors, compilers, anthologizers, even careless scribes or, in the case of oral tradition, social groups, produced a thousand bits of inspired meaning. By further assumptions of critical scholarship each author, editor, compiler and so on directed his literary contribution toward the immediate historical situation in which he found himself. The resultant snippets of text seemed bound to the remote and often unique situations to which they were addressed. The task became to show in what way these texts, each with its own peculiar situation, were related and further to indicate how each escaped the uniqueness of the situation to which it was addressed to achieve the universality required by the concept of divine inspiration.

Besides creating these major problems of fragmentation and particularity, the results of critical scholars' efforts raised a host of minor difficulties requiring adjustments in traditional views. Did a later redactor who changed the sense of a received piece of inspired text by locating it in a new context falsify inspired meaning by departing from the earlier author's intentions? Was every stage in the production of the final biblical text, no matter how trivial or purely mechanical, inspired? If this were the case, then the traditional concept of inspiration of a single author working alone had to be modified to include editors who did no more than join pre-existing sources. On another level, what was one to do with material like Psalm 29? Archaeology had produced an early Ugaritic parallel, making it probable that the crucial psychological moment took place in the mind of a pagan.

Two distinct steps were necessary to meet these problems, and in *The Inspired Word* Alonso-Schökel took them both. First, he broadened the conception of the mechanism of inspiration to accommodate every literary activity which critical scholarship certified to be involved in the composition of the Bible. Whether a social group shaping oral tradition or a self-conscious editor piecing together the Chronicles, all were guided by inspiration, except, of course, the pagan author of Psalm 29. Each stage in the literary process from oral tradition to final book has a psychological component. Consequently, the psychological understanding of the mechanism of inspiration could be broadened relatively easily to include all these different mental activities.

Broadening the range of literary activities that could be inspired resolved many of the minor problems and fit better with the current understanding of the actual process of composition of the Bible. But it did little to defuse the larger threats of fragmentation and particularity. Alonso-Schökel's second step, which is far more interesting and important, moves to counter these problems. In order to solve the problem of the particularity of the individual units of the Bible, Alonso-Schökel argued that in guiding the author, inspiration is oriented toward the production of the final text of Scripture. Inspiration directs the activity of each author, editor, collector, or any other agent who contributes to the literary shape of the text to produce precisely the text which constitutes Scripture. Each individual author might be completely unaware of the final goal. Certainly the earliest authors could not anticipate what was to become of their work. But the Holy Spirit always held the *telos* firmly in sight and directed the author's particularistic efforts toward the ultimate goal.

This distinction between the author's particularistic motives and the broader intentions of the Holy Spirit duplicates precisely the central distinction that gave rise to the *sensus plenior*. And the result is similar in both cases: the human author is displaced by the divine author. The effect is to displace those isolated snippets of text produced by the individual authors with the results of the Holy Spirit's activity, the complete inspired text of Scripture.

To his credit but to our perplexity, Alonso-Schökel follows with consistency the logic of his own argument away from the psychological processes of human composition toward the finished text and the intrinsic mode of criticism's exclusive focus on the literary text. The orientation toward the finished text places him in agreement with contemporary critics:

> Today, however, scholars are agreed that the proper object of literary study is the work itself, and that the study of the author and his epoch in the light of sociology, psychology, the history of ideas, etc., has a place only insofar as it aids in understanding the work.[42]

This position is fully consistent with the reorientation toward the work which results from making the *telos* of the Holy Spirit the dominant force in inspiration. But it makes a shambles of Alonso-Schökel's carefully constructed psychological communication model. All those psychological considerations are irrelevant to the work. Alon-

---

42 Alonso-Schökel, *Inspired Word*, p. 258.

so-Schökel seems struck by the embarrassment caused his earlier interest in the author by this belated conversion to the centrality of the work, but is only able to muster a footnote to his own dramatic statement of authorial irrelevance, protesting some influence of authorial intentions. His argument amounts to no more than the unprovable hypothesis that the intentions of the biblical authors at some points coincided with the broad theological intentions of the Spirit and were therefore incorporated into the text. This amounts to a very modest claim at best. Nothing would be lost interpretatively by disregarding it, as long as it is the intentions of the Holy Spirit that are determinative.

The desire to avoid the dangers of fragmentation and particularism primarily accounts for this abrupt about-face. Ascribing the whole work to the Spirit establishes its literary unity in the same way that ascribing entire biblical books to a single author did formerly. And the problem of particularity simply disappears with the deemphasis of the unique situation of the human author. But there are other advantages. First, the reduced interest in the author corresponds to the lower status of the individuals with which critical scholarship populates the productive process. Reaching great psychological depth may be important when the biblical author is viewed as a single person of deep piety and theological genius. But the interest wanes when we confront a proliferation of authors, editors, collectors, and scribes, faceless individuals engaged often enough in mundane, mechanical operations. Their efforts are incommensurate with the results, and interest naturally pursues the results.

On the more positive side, the emphasis on the inspired nature of the text allows a full, rich literary reading of the work, unfettered by nagging questions of whether meaningful literary effects perceived in the text were intended by the human author or not. All can be attributed purely formally to the Holy Spirit, meaning that in practice the issue of intentions does not arise. As a result, a juxtaposition of two different types of text, which from the point of view of redaction criticism constitutes the purest accident, can be evaluated semantically as an important and meaningful structural feature, perhaps the key to the passage. In effect, directing inspiration toward the finished work stresses its autonomy and allows the sort of intrinsic criticism which treats the text as a "closed stylistic unity." The potential forcefulness of the application of Alonso-Schökel's exegetical methods depends on some principle establishing the work's autonomy. Inspiration directed toward production of the final work supplies the necessary principle.

The autonomy of the text is essential to a full literary reading. And it is crucial to solving the problems of fragmentation and particularity. But Alonso-Schökel purchases it at the cost of a most remarkable and disturbing inconsistency. The inconsistency is exemplified by two quotations taken from adjoining pages of *The Inspired Word*. In the first Alonso-Schökel cites with approval perhaps the most famous *dictum* on authorial irrelevance in recent literature, W. K. Wimsatt's "The poem is not the critic's own and not the author's (it is detached from the author at birth and goes about beyond his power to intend it or control it)."[43] The second quotation is from Alonso-Schökel himself, on the following page: "We might say that in the work and through the work we come into contact with things and events and with the author."[44]

It is not incontestable that these statements are irreconcilable. The author may indeed be found in self-referential sections of a work without compromising its autonomy. But, if "contact with the author" is understood in the sense so carefully developed in the first two-thirds of *The Inspired Word*, according to which a literary work in all its aspects is reduced to the communication of its author's inner life, the contradiction is absolute. Focusing on the author's life subordinates the meaning of the text to the task of understanding the author, destroying the integrity of structural patterns within the text by referring them to external impulses in the mind of the author. On the other hand, maintaining the autonomy of the textual meaning removes the warrant for direct inferences about the author's person. What must be clearly stated is that Alonso-Schökel may not have it both ways simply by ignoring the implications that textual autonomy and authorial centrality have for each other.

The two principles of textual autonomy and the ability of the text to point beyond itself are both essential in order to address the central problems associated with revelation and inspiration in the critical age. But the formulations Alonso-Schökel gives the principles are unsatisfactory. Nowhere is this more apparent than in the case of inspiration. Providing a mental locus for inspiration serves to compromise the

---

43 Ibid., p. 299, quoted from Wimsatt, *The Verbal Icon*, p. 5.
44 Alonso-Schökel, *The Inspired Word*, p. 300.

autonomy of the text. But maintaining the autonomy of the text by considering the finished form inspired removes the author from consideration. And the author is the text's link to the outside world, in Alonso-Schökel's model.

In what we have examined so far of Alonso-Schökel's treatment of revelation and inspiration, no full explanation has emerged of why he favors the psychological theory of language. To understand more completely what is at stake, it is necessary to examine his discussion of the truth and authority of Scripture.

First, a few preliminary remarks. Alonso-Schökel is determined to get beyond the apologetic concerns which have acted as a drag on the development of a positive definition of biblical truth. The penchant of the theological manuals to derive a single principle—inerrancy—from the doctrine of inspiration is hopelessly narrow. He is no more patient with the limitation on Scripture occasioned by considering truth as exclusively a property of logical propositions. That limits Scripture to what can be expressed in syllogistic form. What does not already conform to propositional form or cannot be easily converted assumes an uncertain status. Alonso-Schökel is frustrated by all such limitations.

To escape them, Alonso-Schökel gives the discussion a decisive twist by defining truth ontologically rather than epistemologically:

> In the context of the word "Truth," Christ, Who has revealed God, is the Truth. Not only does He speak the truth, He causes it to be, and is Himself the Truth. In an analogous and participated way, sacred Scripture, insofar as it is the revelation of God, is the truth.
>
> We can think of this in terms of ontological truth: the manifestation of being and of its meaning...[45]

There is a close analogy here with human experience. "When we know a person, we possess the truth of that person in a unified way."[46] But the truth of God is absolute and the standard of all other truth.

This ontological truth is manifested in the actions of God and Christ. Each individual action manifests part of the truth. "He divides His self-manifestation into a long series of salvific acts which give under-

---

45 Ibid., p. 312.
46 Ibid., p. 312.

standing of diverse aspects of His unity."[47] Taken together, the acts form a whole which comprises the complete self-revelation of God.

The psychological communication model fits neatly with this ontological definition of truth. If God is Truth, then the task is to make contact with God in order to know the truth. A central tenet of Alonso-Schökel's literary model is that literature is a form of communication, a channel between the author and reader. In reading Scripture, the Christian contacts Truth in the person of God, not, indeed, as God *in se*, but in the linguistically mediated form which is all we can know of any other individual.

This definition of truth and our relation to it has tremendous appeal. It allows a mediate yet nearly direct access to the embodiment of truth. Further, the model corresponds to the Christian's attitude toward the truth of Scripture. The truth of Scripture is not questioned as is the truth of a proposition but is assumed and then applied to the judgment of other truths. It is for this reason that in actual Christian practice apologetic defense of Scripture is beside the point and, as Alonso-Schökel protests, represents wasted effort. Still further, the definition allows a very broad conception of what is significant about Scripture. The range of significance is not restricted to what may be expressed in propositional form. Every detail of the text is potentially an expression of God's being, and, consequently, significant. The great strength of this is that important aspects of the text, such as its stylistic features, which were overlooked by speculative theology's concentration on propositions, can be reintroduced into theology and into the wider use of Scripture. An unnatural restriction disappears.

There is no denying the importance of reorienting the issue of truth toward the person of God. But the connection of this definition with Alonso-Schökel's specific literary model raises misgivings. We have already seen both theoretical and practical problems with inferences from the literary givens of a text to corresponding impulses in the author. Inferences of this sort may seem appropriate for narrative portions of the New Testament where Scripture does function to reveal the identity of Jesus directly. But the same model has great difficulty with the literary complexity of the Old Testament. A somewhat unfair

---

47 Ibid., p. 313.

question will illustrate the problem. What inference could we draw about God's being from the story of the destruction of Ai? If we proceed on the same lines as we would, for instance, in drawing inferences from Jesus' healing of the lepers, the necessary inference is that God is ruthless and bloodthirsty. Obviously, this is unacceptable. But how is the inference to be avoided? If, as Alonso-Schökel argued, the tone of a piece is the objectified mood of its author, it if is a communication of its author's experience, then can the cold-blooded account of slaughter be taken otherwise than as implying a dire moral insensitivity on the part of the author of Joshua 8 and, following the chain of causality back but one more step, on the part of God?

The question is perhaps unfair because virtually any reading of Joshua 8 will be troubled by the flat moral tone. But Alonso-Schökel's model seems particularly prone to encourage premature and false inferences about the author from details of the story. And in cases such as Joshua 8 in which such inferences are obviously inappropriate, the model lacks any clear principles indicating why the inferences are out of place.

The great weakness here lies in the inflexibility and fundamental inappropriateness of the model of literature as essentially a mode of communication between author and reader. Alonso-Schökel pushes the communication model very hard in order to establish that the meaning of the biblical text represents the communication of God's being, of Truth, and is therefore itself true and absolutely authoritative. Alonso-Schökel extends the communication model to virtually every facet of the literary text, so that every literary effect has a correlate in the experience of the author. Viewed from the side of the text, this means that every literary feature of the text communicates some aspect of the author's experience or being. The directness of the correlation between text and experience certainly strengthens the link between the biblical text and Truth. But when we begin with the meaning of individual texts, as we normally do, and then make inferences about the author's experience, the very directness of the inference raises serious problems.

The corrective to the inflexibility of the communications model and the overly direct inferences about the author it engenders is to stress the autonomy of the text, its integrity independent of the author. As we have seen, Alonso-Schökel does also affirm the principle of the autonomy of the meaning of the text. But the principle of autonomy does not allow the biblical text to derive its truth from the ontological Truth of its author. Another type of truth must be defined which is appropriate to the autonomous character of the text's meaning. Alonso-Schökel therefore defines a "truth properly literary," within which there is a division between a primary and secondary truth. "The *primary truth* is the internal coherence of a work which reveals truth to us as a property of being, and as such makes an appeal to the person."[48] By associating truth with literary coherence and the ability of the work to make an appeal to the person, Alonso-Schökel provides principles at once properly literary, broad enough to apply to all forms of literature, and sufficiently determinate to provide criteria to distinguish true from false.

Yet Alonso-Schökel immediately moves to restrict the principle. In an example he argues that many of the kings of Israel are unconvincing as characters. The deuteronomistic historian reduces them to types (good king, bad king), not full-blown characters with all the complexity and depth their real-life alter egos must have had. Because these biblical types do not correspond to real life, Alonso-Schökel is prepared to admit that they are unconvincing; they lack literary truth.

The assumptions that lie behind this judgment are characteristic of Alonso-Schökel. The coherence of the literary text is judged not by its correspondence to human experience broadly understood, but by its faithful correspondence to a specific external reality, the character to which the text refers. It is assumed that for literature to be convincing, it must be mimetic. This is certainly a very restrictive assumption, far more restrictive than one's normal experience of literature would support. It seems to involve a thoroughgoing confusion between convincing and realistic, truth and verisimilitude.

The requirement that convincing literature be mimetic seems related to an earlier statement expressing the relationship of text to experience. "The text incorporates an experience, personal or otherwise, presents it authentically or truly, and is able to evoke an authentic decision."[49] Experience stands at the center; this is the heart of Alonso-Schökel's earlier theory of truth, here thrust into the middle of a discussion of literary truth. The text is a direct conversion of experience into language. The most faithful conversion into language will most

---

48 Ibid., pp. 316-317.
49 Ibid., p. 317.

closely mirror the original experience. In the case of historical experience like that of the kings of Israel, the most faithful conversion will be mimetic.

The implication is that authors such as the deuteronomistic historians who write nonmimetic accounts have failed to convert experience into language; the language does not recognizably correspond to the experience and as a result it is unconvincing. The end of this line of reasoning, though, is the destruction of "truth properly literary." Real truth in this model lies only in the original experience and, derivatively, in the text's ability to mimic it. Judgment of literary truth is reduced to a judgment whether the literary account actually corresponds to its underlying experience. This is a severely attenuated concept of literary truth, since the truth of the literary work is directly dependent on nonliterary experience.

The secondary truth of literature is difficult to describe, though familiar to all experienced readers. Alonso-Schökel begins: "A literary work presents to us new aspects of reality and experience, broadening our knowledge by acquaintance."[50] The literary work creates a world into which the reader is drawn. The reader who enters that world gains knowledge of it by direct experience. It is appropriate to say that the "new aspects of reality and experience" encountered in the text are true, and that the new knowledge gained by acquaintance with them is equally true.

This truth of literature is secondary only in the sense that it depends on literary coherence as a necessary precondition. In relation to literary experience, it is primary and constitutes what we commonly mean when we judge a literary work true. The ultimate truth of a literary work is proven when the truth given by experience of the world of the text confronts previous experience. Then that truth can force a decision and change a life:

> A work of literature reveals our own meaning and depth and makes us conscious of ourselves. As we read, we see ourselves in the light of the author or

---

50 Ibid., p. 318.

of his work, and in virtue of this knowledge we can respond by acting to change ourselves.[51]

The final truth of a literary work is testified to by its ability to illicit a decision to bring one's life into conformity with the reality it presents. What is the relationship between the world created within the text and the world outside the text? For the existentialists to whom Alonso-Schökel is indebted, the textual world is completely independent of the outside world; it constitutes an independent reality.[52] The reality originates in actual events and represents a direct conversion of those events. The mechanism for this direct conversion is described in Alonso-Schökel's psycholinguistic theory. The important fact for the issue of the ontology of the text is that the linguistic process originates in actual events and proceeds by unbroken stages to the final text. In the process, the highest ontological status held by events is lost. But in the nature of the case, this is unavoidable. The immediacy of events is ephemeral, gone the instant the event passes. There can be no immediate experience of the events underlying the biblical text. But, by virtue of the unbroken chain stretching from it to original events, the final text can claim to represent an ontologically secondary form of the events. Secondary status involves no denigration of authority or reality in this system, because the primary events are irretrievably gone.

For its part, the text derives its reality from events. On the other side, the events take on meaning only when converted to intelligible, communicable form. As Alonso-Schökel puts it, "In the Scriptures an historical event, unique and irreversible, is presented in its inner meaning..."[53] "An event presented in this way unlocks the mystery of its meaning, and transcends its own limitations."[54] Events receive their meaning in being converted to language and assume a permanent, communicable form.

The dialectic between text and external world, most importantly, God's being, clarifies what has been at stake in the constant referen-

51 Ibid.

52 Alonso-Schökel cites Hans Meyerhoff, *Time in Literature* (Berkeley: University of California Press, 1955) as the immediate source of this discussion; ibid., p. 315.

53 Ibid., p. 319.

54 Ibid.

ces to the author, to historical and psychological events, and to the psycholinguistic theory. In this conception the text depends on its unbroken genetic relationship to events for its reality and for its claim to pertain to the actual world. Its claim to be taken seriously, indeed with ultimate seriousness, rests on the ultimate nature of the events behind it and its correspondence to them. Further, the text's authority and truth are made dependent on the integrity of the chain linking the final text to the ultimate source of truth and authority in God. There is little wonder that Alonso-Schökel construes that link as closely and directly as he does.

But in forging such a firm genetic chain in order to establish the ontological status of the text and its foundation in the ultimate reality of God, Alonso-Schökel has incurred methodological inconsistencies and flawed interpretations of individual texts. The problems that have appeared repeatedly in this survey seem unavoidable given this conception. It might seem that considering the events themselves inchoate would remove them from consideration and allow a consistent focus on the meaning of the text. But the force of that strong genetic link at the heart of the literary theory is again and again to return the interpreter to a concern with the events themselves as explanations of the literary givens in the text. The result is a confusion in method between extrinsic and intrinsic techniques of analysis, a confusion, even outright conflict, between the course of events and the meaning of the text, and a reduction of the text to the scope of the events that can be established behind it. Pressing the "events" side of the dialectic relationship in practice subordinates the independent meaning of the text to events, compromising the text's independence.

Conclusion

Alonso-Schökel's work is complex and broad and it evokes complex responses. Foremost is recognition of the advance made in adopting a literary model, focusing attention on the biblical text as the locus of revelation and inspiration, highlighting the features of the text that give it power in the liturgy and in private meditation. Alonso-Schökel's work amounts to a major and positive reorientation of biblical scholarship and, although he is not alone in announcing the reorientation, he is among the most prominent, especially in Catholic circles.

But alongside recognition of Alonso-Schökel's achievement in opening new avenues of interpretation must be some dismay at the contradiction that pierces and compromises his work. Understanding the important doctrinal issues that Alonso-Schökel seeks to balance cannot dispel the feeling that he has not succeeded in finding the proper balance point. The contradictions unsettle all confidence in Alonso-Schökel's positive contributions.

I have tried to show that Alonso-Schökel operates with two central hermeneutical principles, the autonomy of the meaning of the text and the ability of the text to refer outside itself, and that these two principles are used to address particular theological problems involving Scripture. It is an important fact that most of Alonso-Schökel's positive contributions are associated with the first principle. The autonomy of the text successfully opposes the reduction of the text to a sequence of historical facts or a compendium of doctrinal propositions. A much broader, more flexible use of Scripture results. The autonomy of the text further avoids the boondoggle of "inerrancy" by resisting the identification of the truth of the literary text with its correspondence to historical events. The autonomy of the text allows Scripture to be interpreted as a unity. Distinctions of authorship, historical versus non-historical background, original versus redactional, early versus late, while all unquestionably valid as descriptions of the process by which the text was produced, do not provide grounds to distinguish degrees of authority or inspiration within Scripture. The final text is all equally inspired. Finally, the autonomy of the text accords with Scripture's traditional dignity as the locus of revelation. Scripture itself is revelation, not the events behind it.

It is an equally important fact that most of the problems encountered in the course of this study arose from the second principle, the referentiality of the text or its connection with the outside world. Alonso-Schökel consistently attempted to tie the meaning of the text as firmly as possible to the reality of the extratextual world. Pushing the connection so hard created problems in two areas. First, the meaning of the text came into open conflict with the demands of the logic of historical discourse. The obvious meaning of Genesis 2-3 cannot be coordinated with actual historical events by normal historical demonstration. Insisting on a connection forced Alonso-Schökel to distort the normal rules and procedures of historical method in order to make room within them for the meaning of the text. Second, the literary effects in the text resist direct correlation either to events in the outside world or to aspects of the author's psychology. We simply do not refer such literary effects as tone to the psychology of the author but integrate them thematically with other literary elements to produce meaning in the text. The obvious meaning of a text such as Hosea 1-3 stands in judgment of any reconstruction of external event which does not agree with it and not the other way around.

These difficulties indicate that on both historical and literary grounds, Alonso-Schökel has connected the text too firmly to the outside world. In effect he has put too much stress on the principle of referentiality of the text, pushing it to the point of direct conflict with the principle of the autonomy of the text. At the center of Alonso-Schökel's hermeneutical system is a drastic contradiction because he has not yet worked out a theory of the referentiality of the text to the outside world which is compatible with the autonomy and integrity of meaning of a literary work. He has simply transposed the logic of referentiality appropriate to historical texts and face-to-face communication to the quite different area of literary texts. We have seen the unsatisfactory results. Nonetheless, on the side of the autonomy of the text, Alonso-Schökel has made decisive advances. But the question of the relationship of the autonomous text to the outside world is still open.

Chapter 4

Norbert Lohfink

Norbert Lohfink concludes a survey of Catholic exegetes' "love-hate" relationship with historical criticism: "I myself belong to a generation which no longer has to struggle to justify these methods. For us they are self-evident. To speak of their sense or necessity bores us."[1] Boredom with the issue was new. Earlier Catholic scholars, even well into this century, contended with an anticritical legacy bequeathed by an earlier age. One troubling part of that legacy was the unfortunate union, concluded in the late Middle Ages, between the dogmatic definition of inspiration and the popular, uncritical understanding of biblical authorship then current, according to which each book had a single, renowned biblical figure as author. God inspired these authors, thereby inspiring the books they produced. This conception of unitary, inspired authorship was associated in a natural way with a holistic reading of the biblical books. Each section of a book could be read in conjunction with all other sections on the same level.

Initially, critical scholarship directly challenged only the uncritical assumption of unitary authorship. But in the controversy between the earlier biblical interpretation and the new, the doctrine of inspiration and the holistic reading of Scripture, the whole earlier system, were interlocked with the theory of unitary authorship. Inspiration was drawn into the fight to provide an explanation and rationale for the unity of the text. Once inspiration was bound up with unitary authorship as its validating principle, the challenge of critical scholarship was fundamental. Generations of Catholic scholars played out the consequences of linking inspiration and the traditional holistic reading with the

---

1 Norbert Lohfink, "Katholische Bibelwissenschaft und historischkritische Methode," *Stimmen der Zeit* 177/5 (1966), p. 336.

critically vulnerable hypothesis of single authorship, forced to resist critical scholarship and its penetration into the origins of the biblical text in defense of the inspiration of Scripture and the continued validity of traditional readings. The largely unreflective connection made in the Middle Ages between inspiration and single authorship became the main battleground, with the holistic reading a hostage to the conflict.

By the early twentieth century the critical tide had broken over Catholic scholars. As Lohfink says, "Anyone who did not want to violate his conscience had to enter the scholarly underground."[2] The weight of evidence supporting composite authorship was irresistible to anyone prepared to consider it seriously. In the intellectual climate of the twentieth century, it was a self-exiling decision to ignore the historical evidence.

The triumph of critical scholarship swept away the hypothesis of single authorship, which was clearly untenable. Because the holistic reading of Scripture had been interlocked with the theory of single authorship, it too was largely swept away. The holistic reading's claim to validity was traditionally premised on unitary authorship. When critical research removed this premise, the holistic reading was left without a validating principle. Historical criticism did not interpret the text holistically, but divided it according to historical strata, so that locating a unifying principle within historical criticism was unlikely. In any case, the triumph of historical criticism was so total that criticism defined and limited the area within which a principle in support of a holistic reading could be sought. Any effort to reestablish the holistic reading would have to be based on historical principles subject to verification by critical means. For Lohfink and his generation, trained after *Divino Afflante Spiritu*, beyond but still very close to the struggle to have critical methods recognized, this limitation to historical principles was a fundamental premise of responsible scholarship. There was no return to any part of the old system of interpretation except along the path laid down by historical criticism.

The change in the conventions governing valid interpretation does not alone explain the depth of the conversion of Lohfink's generation of scholars to historical critical methods. Historical criticism brought

---

2 Ibid., p. 334.

real illumination into the dark background of the biblical text. Lohfink tells of one of his professors who conducted class according to an invariable formula. The students were instructed to turn to a particularly obscure biblical passage. The professor reviewed the suggestions of Church Fathers and modern scholars, he solicited the students' own suggestions, all without cutting through the interpretive crux. Then, *deus ex machina*, the professor produced a text from Ugarit containing the same or similar words in a fuller context. The sense of the biblical text became clear. The historical method proved itself in bringing light into an obscure corner of the text. The larger benefit was clear. As Lohfink says, "The illuminated past is a piece of better controlled reality."[3]

Lohfink's commitment to historical criticism, both as intellectually responsible methodology and welcome means to deeper insight, is deeply rooted. Yet he also recognizes the limitations of historical criticism. At the center of historical research lies a paradox. The new light shed by research on the biblical world actually increases the darkness and in a number of ways. Most obvious is that all new knowledge reveals how much remains to be known. The point of illumination plays across a background of darkness not perceived until the first ray of light penetrated it. Lohfink refers to the Qumran texts, which revealed a sect virtually unknown before the finds. Knowledge of the existence of the sect brought questions about its nature, as well as a fresh and painful reminder of the vast amounts of textual matter that was not so fortunately preserved. "With light came darkness."[4]

Better understanding of the nature of the historical sources coming from the biblical period has increased our apprehension of their imprecision. Nowhere do we find historical reports approaching modern canons of accuracy. Most of the genres represented in biblical literature and the literature of Israel's neighbors are not typified by their strong interest in precise historical detail.

Appreciation of the amount of pertinent information lost and the imprecision of the sources that are available leads to recognition of the necessarily hypothetical character of all historical reconstructions. The

3 Ibid., p. 337.
4 Ibid., p. 337.

data the historian marshals in support of one reconstruction can be organized into other patterns. New information may require still unforeseen reconstructions. To the historian, the hypothetical nature of his reconstructions is simply a given. The historian's task is to expand or modify the hypothesis to cover more data and continually to search for new information. It is necessary to be open to the necessity of modifying or abandoning the hypothesis as new information becomes available. Abandoning a hypothesis is not failure but progress, an essential step to better understanding.

The theologian's, especially the biblical theologian's, attitude toward the hypothetical nature of historical reconstructions is less sanguine. Scripture is the fundament of the life of faith. So long as the correct understanding of Scripture depends on historical reconstructions, the center of faith remains hypothetical. Protestant theologians have attempted to make a virtue of this situation by seeing it as a salutary check on dogmatism. Catholic scholars most recently have tended to see it as an unavoidable consequence of the divine word being given in human form. All human knowledge, even of the absolute reality of God, is tentative and hypothetical. These considerations have their weight, but the situation is still troubling to one such as Lohfink who, as both theologian and historian, surveys the sharply diverging currents of modern critical scholarship, currents that rise and fall, shift, mingle, separate again. The historian need not be concerned, but the theologian seeking a firm basis for faith can only react with alarm.

The very success of the method imposes other limits on historical criticism. Historical information can inhibit the full play of biblical images. Ezekiel's vision of the heavenly entourage, described vividly yet enigmatically, is reduced by referring the reader to the winged colossi in the Louvre or British Museum for the prototypes. Specification does not always enhance the effect of images.

The success of the method also increases the distance lying between the reader and text. The more the events portrayed in the text are firmly located in a culture differing radically from our own, the more remote and consequently irrelevant those events may seem. The success of historical investigation opens a chasm which the theologian is left to bridge.

The alien quality of reconstructed historical situations is not a problem for the historian. It too may be given a positive value, liberating past events from modern thought patterns, the result a broadening of our own thought. Nor is the restriction in imagery resulting from

making symbolic words concrete properly the historian's concern.
Lohfink recognizes that the historian has different interests than the
exegete and, in fact, parlays this recognition into two distinctions
designed to mark off the exegete's proper area of interest without
severing the methodological link between exegesis and historical
criticism. Lohfink's first distinction is between historical methods and
the historical question.[5] The historical question, simply stated, is
"What happened?" "The historical question is the question how it really was."[6] Historical method, on the other hand, is "a limited number of
techniques, aids, and rules which serve to answer the historical question scientifically."[7] Historical methods may be used to answer the historical question proper, but their application is not restricted to that
single question. Historical methods are instruments that may be
employed in many areas of work.

The distinction between historical method and historical question is
preliminary, though necessary, if "history" is not to be limited to the
historical question alone. The more important distinction is between
history proper and explication or exegesis (*Auslegung*) of a text. Lohfink illutrates the distinction very clearly. Considering a Platonic
dialogue, one can ask the historical question. Did it actually take place?
Even if it did not, additional historical questions are still in order. Does
the text accurately represent the character of Socrates and the nature
of his discourses? These questions belong to history proper. But there
is a completely different problematic if one begins to ask "what the text
actually wants to say,"[8] to enter into dialogue with the content of the
text itself, to "philosophize with Plato."[9] Then the purely historical
question of what happened is subsidiary to the question of meaning. It
is the assertions (*Aussage*) made by the text, its sense or import, which
is properly the interest of the exegete. Exegete and historian share the
same text, but their interests in it differ. The exegete is concerned with
meaning, the historian with the text's relation to historical event. Con-

---

5 Ibid., p. 340.
6 Ibid.
7 Ibid.
8 Ibid., p. 340.
9 Ibid.

sequently, the exegete and the historian address different questions to the text, the exegete wanting to know what it says in itself, the historian what it says about a historical situation.

Despite the different questions addressed to the text, Lohfink maintains, history and explication are closely related. There is a "reciprocal relation of dependence" between the two.[10] The historian requires a full and accurate understanding of the sense of the text as a basis for historical inferences about actual situations. In turn, the exegete only correctly understands the text when he knows the circumstances of its composition and its relation to historical fact.[11]

The reciprocal relation, however, is complete in only a very few types of text. In eyewitness accounts of events, for one instance, the question of what really happened and what the text means coincide very closely. This is the limiting case of coincidence. In most texts, including biblical texts, there are many assertions which do not depend on prior historical knowledge to be understood but are plain in their sense on first reading. In the same texts may be other assertions which do require historical information. Proportions between the types of assertions vary from genre to genre and even within texts of the same genre. Lohfink's distinction between history, which is concerned with events, and explication, which is concerned with textual assertions, whether about events or not, allows those assertions not dependent on historical information full weight as the legitimate object of explication. This represents a significant, even radical, departure from the practice of most historical critics, who focus primarily on that part of the text's assertions clearly related to history. They ask the historical question in many forms first. Lohfink asks the question of meaning first and finds that it is possible in many instances to grasp a text's assertions, to "philosophize with Plato," with relatively little reference to historical issues. Under these circumstances explication is a historical question "only in a very derivative sense."[12]

The immediate advantage of beginning with meaning, the assertions of the text, rather than the historical question, is to reduce the severity of the problems associated with history. The darkness that accom-

10 Ibid., p. 341.
11 Ibid., p. 340.
12 Ibid.

panies new historical knowledge is of peripheral concern so long as the assertions of the text are understood. The actual assertions of the biblical text are not remote, any more than the arguments in a Platonic dialogue. The meaning of the text is directly before the reader. Despite the historical distance to Plato, the reader is directly confronted by his ideas and arguments and can, indeed must, wrestle with them as immediate issues. The theological process employing biblical texts is similar, because the assertions of the text are theologically normative, not the history behind them. Lohfink is unequivocal on this important point. However, in the theological use of biblical texts, unlike Platonic dialogues, the demand is not to enter into argument with the assertions of the text but to appropriate them. "The appropriation of the contentual assertions of the texts as one's own assertions is what is called belief."[13]

Lohfink is registering here what I earlier called, in reference to Alonso-Schökel's work, the autonomy of meaning of the text. The meaning of the text is independent of the historical circumstances of its composition. And Lohfink uses the principle in a similar way to establish an area of textual meaning which is not constricted by historical questions and the limits of the historicist viewpoint. But for Lohfink the principle of autonomy and the distinction between history and explication based on it are only designed to reduce the historical problems, not remove them entirely. To remove all historical problems would demand a clear break with historical method which Lohfink opposes. History is always and necessarily hypothetical because it must always be open to modification by new information or its own changing problematic. Openness to reformulation is a structural feature of historical writing, a highly positive feature because it allows the incorporation of new knowledge. Exegesis, to the extent it wants to be historical—and this is very important to Lohfink's generation—must share that openness and the resultant hypothetical character of its interpretations. Room is left for this proper historical interest in the recognition that some of the assertions of the text are dependent on historical information in order to be understood.

13 Ibid., p. 341.

In giving priority to the question of meaning over the historical question and in maintaining that some of the assertions — the meaning — of the text are independent of historical knowledge, Lohfink enters uncharted waters, seemingly unaware. Lohfink continues to rely predominately on historical categories and reasoning, despite the fact that they are only appropriate to those assertions of the text dependent on historical information. What seems to be demanded is some theoretical reflection on the nature of the process of understanding those assertions of the text which are not dependent on historical information but are understood directly or immediately. What processes are involved, what methodologies aid the process, and what checks are there against false or willful readings? Further, since some of the assertions are understood directly, others only after historical preparation, the question naturally arises of the relation of the two types of assertion, of priority, compatibility, and method of combination. Lohfink does not offer any theoretical discussion of these most important issues and it is necessary to turn to his exegetical work to find, if not direct answers, at least general indications of his approach to them. An early work, "Der Bundesschluss im Land Moab: Redaktionsgeschichtliches zu Dt 28, 69-32, 47," is typical and illustrates particularly the change in emphasis from historical questions to the assertions of the text itself.[14]

Lohfink begins his considerations with an observation made over a hundred years ago by Paul Kleinert[15] that the book of Deuteronomy is subdivided by four superscriptions: 1:1 "These are the words"; 4:44 "and this is the law"; 28:69 "These are the words of the covenant"; and 33:1 "And this is the blessing." The superscriptions are obviously

---

14 Norbert Lohfink, "Der Bundesschluss im Land Moab: Redaktionsgeschichtliches zu Dt 28, 69-32, 47," *Biblische Zeitschrift* NF 6 (1962), pp. 32-56.

15 Paul Kleinert, *Das Deuteronomium und der Deuteronomiker* (Bielefeld and Leipzig: J. C. Hinrich, 1872), p. 167.

redactional, a fact that led to their long neglect by scholars preoccupied with earlier, more "original" aspects of Deuteronomy. Lohfink proposes to give the superscriptions, particularly 28:69, serious attention. If it can be shown that the superscriptions are appropriate to the material they introduce and are not extraneous glosses and irrelevancies, then they may lay claim to a greater interpretive value than any alternate system for organizing the material of Deuteronomy advanced by critical scholars: "they offer a self-explication of the text, are themselves text."[16] They constitute assertions of the text itself which must be decisive against all outside categories. If the superscription in 28:69 is to be credited and not taken as a casual appurtenance, Lohfink must demonstrate two things:[17] first, that the four chapters from 28:69-32:47 are in some fashion a unity which can be subsumed under a single superscription, and second, that the superscription, "These are the words of the covenant," is in some way appropriate to the whole unit.

There is no question of recourse to source critical/literary critical criteria to demonstrate the unity of the chapters. They clearly do not derive from a single source. The Song of Moses in Ch. 32 is easily distinguished from the material in 29-30, for example, and fine divisions can be made within 28-30 itself. The unifying factor, rather, lies in the activity of the redactor who brought the distinct sources together to construct a meaningful whole.

To support the case for significant redactional activity, Lohfink points to intentional structural features within the four chapters which cross literary critical lines and serve to join distinct subsections together and to signal the meaning of the whole. The structural features are of two types. First are stylistic features which were composed by the author or redactor for this specific context. The superscription itself is one example, but Lohfink also finds chiasms, progressive subdivisions, systematic alternation in the length of subunits, pointed use

---

16 Lohfink, "Bundesschluss," p. 34.

17 Lohfink calls for a reappraisal of the contribution of redactors. In earlier periods their additions were described in metaphors drawn from the unconscious growth of plants or side-branching of streams. There was often the none-too-subtle intimation of the perversion of original purity. Lohfink suggests that more appropriate metaphors could be drawn from architecture, the redactor consciously building with preformed material, creating a rational order. See ibid., p. 34.

of vocabulary, and allusions to other texts. The second type of structure is provided by literary *Gattungen* which were fixed in their form before the redactor employed them to shape his text. The decision to use one particular *Gattung* rather than some other as the structural model represents a conscious, meaningful choice by the author or redactor. But the specific structural configuration the *Gattung* bears is independent of the redactor, produced, according to the form-critical hypothesis, in a preliterary period of use in an actual social situation. Lohfink cites the covenant formulary described by George Mendenhall and Klaus Baltzer as the structural model which, in a somewhat modified form, provides the dominant structuring device for the four chapters.[18]

Both types of structuring devices, stylistic and formal, appear in Lohfink's argument to similar effect. In the first stage of his argument, which is concerned to show the extent of the material joined together in a single unit, Lohfink takes the presence of structural features, whether stylistic or formal, to indicate that all the material encompassed by the structuring device belongs to a single unit. The specific rationale for this conclusion which moves from the presence of structural features to unity differs slightly between stylistic and formal features. The stylistic argument is absolutely direct. To recognize structure is to recognize the coherence of all the parts that comprise it. Put negatively, it is not possible to deny the unity of a complex structure without denying its existence. Designating a textual sequence A-B-B'-A' a chiasm in itself recognizes the coherence of the unit. Lohfink adds a step to this argument by identifying the stylistic device with the author/redactor's intentions, assuming that what lies behind the literary unity is a unifying consciousness. This step is not analytically necessary and the structure of the argument is essentially single staged, from direct perception of stylistic structure to the unity entailed by that perception. The argument involving either citation of pre-existent material or formal dependence on a fixed *Gattung* involves two stages.

---

18 The frequency with which Lohfink refers to the covenant formulary in much of his work, not just this article, needs to be noted. Mendenhall's and Baltzer's comparative studies made a deep impression on Lohfink, contributing to his conviction of the efficacy and necessity of historical research.

In these cases the unifying structure is not perceived immediately within the text itself. To recognize that a particular passage contains a citation of another text, one must be familiar with the text cited. To recognize a fixed formal structure in a text, one must be familiar with the independent formal model with its regular sequence of formal elements. For scholarly purposes, the existence of the fixed model must be demonstrated convincingly. Then, in a second stage, the formal elements of the text under consideration can be compared to the established structural model. In the specific case of Deuteronomy 29-32 Lohfink accepts the work of Mendenhall and Baltzer as demonstrating a *Gattung* of treaty or covenant exhibiting the well-known formal elements preamble, antecedent history, stipulations, and so on. The second step is to show that Deuteronomy 29-32 exhibits similar formal elements to the treaty and may therefore be considered a unity. In execution this second step runs into some opposition from the text. The structure of the four chapters does not follow treaty form precisely, with the result that Lohfink must say that Deuteronomy 29-32 is modelled on a *Gattung*, itself modelled on the treaty. The need to adjust the argument raises a warning flag but does not affect the line of argument. Recognition of structure is not immediate but contingent on independent demonstration of the structural model, and a second stage is necessary to establish the parallel between text and model.[19]

Running alongside the issue whether the four chapters constitute a structural unity is the question whether they form a sense unit, so that the superscription, "These are the words of the covenant," applies to them appropriately and as a whole. Addressing this issue involves determining the meaning of the text. To present the meaning, Lohfink relies heavily on analysis of the structural features of the text, both stylistic and, to a larger extent, formal. This attention to structure is again consistent with the weight laid on the assertions of the text itself,

---

19 One may question whether the stylistic argument is completely single staged. A model of what constitutes a chiasm, for instance, to which the text can be compared seems required. And some demonstration of the appropriateness of that model is necessary. See the disagreement between Casanowicz and Alonso-Schökel. Lohfink seems to feel that stylistic devices are self-evident.

with the structural features seen as the key to the point the text wants to make. The analysis of structure, particularly stylistic features, is also reminiscent of Alonso-Schökel's work, although Lohfink is more circumspect than Alonso-Schökel. Lohfink, for example, does not ascribe a specific semantic value to any isolated feature but only to complexes of features and even then using relatively broad terms. Referring to Deuteronomy 29:1-14, Lohfink says, "stylistically, ceremoniality rules,"[20] and then invites attention to a number of features: a pointed sequence of addresses, from the nation to a singular "you" and back to the nation; a five-member chiasm involving prominent and distinctive groupings of words; the use of the word *hayyom* five times as a structural signal to mark off the members of the chiasm. These features taken together create a sense of ceremony or ritual. The tone of the passage is then a highly pertinent factor in determining the meaning of the passage.

There is a difference between saying that a whole complex of stylistic devices creates a sense of ceremony and that the use of long a's and o's symbolizes majesty. Still, Lohfink's assertions raise some of the same issues as Alonso-Schökel's more radical method. Foremost is, how does he know? Again, Lohfink is not reflective on this question and does not present an explicit theoretical treatment of the method by which he arrives at his characterization of stylistic features. The assumption, however, seems to be of an identity between the literary conventions of the redactor and the contemporary reader. The conventions of the text are recognized by their analogy to our own. Changes of addressee and highly structured formal language are characteristic of ceremonies, now and, presumably, then. We found reason to question this assumption when it was made by Alonso-Schökel and the same skepticism is appropriate here. It is, however, necessary to be very clear on the point at which skepticism is warranted. The issue is not whether "ceremonial" is an accurate characterization of our present understanding of the nature of the text. By our conventions, the text is ceremonial and that perception naturally enters our reading of it. The issue Lohfink raises is a historical one, whether that characterization is accurate as a description of the tone of the text in

---

20 Ibid., p. 39.

the historical period in which its redactor composed it. Because we do not know as a matter of fact the full conventions that governed "ceremoniality" in that historic period, we do not know that the passage was intended or perceived as ceremonial. Our own perceptions cannot be projected backward into the earlier time without some warrant. The assumption of an analogy of conventions is inadequate to allow a direct reading of stylistic features using our own literary sensibilities.

Deriving meaning from formal features is, again, less direct than from stylistic devices. The formal structure of Deuteronomy 29-32 is related to the structure of ancient Near Eastern treaties. Or, to be more precise, Lohfink argues they are modelled on a cultic covenant ceremony itself patterned on treaty form. This takes account of parenetic and homiletic elements in Deuteronomy 29-32 not found in treaties. From their actual use in concrete situations, treaties derive a conceptual field which is carried over into the text when the redactor chooses to use the treaty form.[21] Specifically, ancient treaty form carries with it the conceptual categories of a formal, legal relationship, conditional on the lesser partner's faithfulness to obligations placed on him, with rewards or sanctions dependent on that faithfulness. The redactor's choice of the treaty form, even in a derivative manifestation, makes these specific concepts part of the assertion of the text and therefore obviously of major import to the exegete whose primary task is to explicate the text's own assertions. The conceptual world of the treaty also fits closely with the superscription, "These are the words of the covenant," justifying the attention paid to the superscription and confirming the text's own explicit assertion that it is to be taken as a covenant.

The importance of selecting the redaction of the text as the appropriate level of analysis in Lohfink's concern with the assertion of the text needs to be noted. Working at the redactional level allows virtually the whole text to come into consideration, because redaction is nearly the last stage in the production of the final text. Further, focus-

---

21 Lohfink's redaction-critical assumption is that the redactor made a conscious literary decision to use treaty form in order to appropriate the conceptual world of the treaty. The emphasis is on the contribution of the form to the meaning of the text.

ing on the redaction allows many different aspects of the text to be evaluated simultaneously for their contribution to the meaning of the text. Other methodologies restrict the data considered and express conclusions narrowly in categories rooted in the assumptions of the method. Form criticism, for instance, pays particular attention to structural elements and refers the features of the text it discovers to the *Sitz im Leben* in which the *Gattung* was formed. A single mode of explanation is preferred. But the assumption in redaction criticism is that the redactor reigned sovereign over his material. He could use preformed material unchanged, could modify it, add to it, or create new text whole cloth. No single mode of explanation can be assumed to explain all of the redactor's activity, with the result that there is great flexibility to follow the meaning of the text itself and still remain within the bounds of redaction critical method. The danger of undervaluing a semantically important feature simply because a particular methodology does not focus on it, although the text itself does, is reduced. By the simple expedient of attributing everything to the intentions of the redactor, redaction criticism is able to extend its view to take in all of what Lohfink would call the assertions of the text, although it must be noted that redaction criticism is not only concerned with the meaning of those assertions but also with the means by which they were produced.

The redactor, then, is the key link to historical methodologies. The redactor is a personality of the past, fixed in a historical period, so that the reconstruction of his activities and their literary results, the text, is formally historical. More directly, the redactor provides a channel through which historically conditioned material, whether content or form, finds its way into the text. Treaty form, or the covenant ceremony Lohfink postulates as dependent on it, existed independently before the composition of Deuteronomy 29-32. It is through the redactor that the material found its way into the text. The redactor is the contact point between the historical situation and the text, which is so important in Lohfink's effort to balance history and textual meaning.

There is very real strength in Lohfink's redactional approach, especially in its flexibility and the greater attention that can be paid to the literary features of the text. But there are several characteristic vulnerabilities which accompany the method. The first concerns the stylistic devices. There is an underlying question whether every structural phenomenon one can discern in the text can be considered a stylistic feature with either direct semantic significance or even any implication for the unity of the segment of the text in which it is found. Close analysis of any relatively extensive segment of text can discover hundreds of structural patterns, as modern structuralist critics have demonstrated. All are objectively in the text as a matter of descriptive fact. But are all significant; that is, do they all contribute to the meaning of the text? If not, how are we to know which are and which are not significant? This last is the methodologically important question. An answer can be formulated for the modern reader by making explicit conventions of reading which are employed in the act of reading and which govern it, though they are not conscious at the moment one is reading a text. But as a historical hypothesis about what devices were intended to be significant in a remote period, the matter is much more complicated and less susceptible to convincing demonstration simply because the historian is forced to hypothesize the conventions governing usage in that age or resort to the assumption that conventions were similar to those of his own period. Taking one of Lohfink's own examples will illustrate the problem. Lohfink finds a concentric structure within Deuteronomy 30:1-10:

A 1f Protasis	The people repent and heed Yahweh's voice, according to Moses' command
B 3-6 Apodosis	Catchword *swb*, said by Yahweh Reference to ancestors
C 7 Still apodosis	
D 8 Protasis	The center, catchwords as in A
C' 9a Apodosis	
B' 9b Still apodosis	Catchwords as in B
A' 10 Protasis	Catchwords as in A and D

Such a pattern is not implausible, although the high level of abstraction involved invites caution. But the real nature of the problem becomes clearer if we recognize that, using Lohfink's own categories, a quite different structure can be seen.

A 1f Protasis	People repent
B 3-7 Apodosis	*swb* patriarchs
A' 8 Protasis	Catchwords as in A
B' 9 Apodosis	Catchwords as in B
A" 10 Protasis	Catchwords as in A

Instead of a concentric structure, what emerges is a series of conditional sentences related by theme and vocabulary.

The issue here is not which of these suggested structures is right or wrong but the prior question of how we would know. Lohfink has ventured—and this is certainly to his credit—into a very complicated region of interpretation. Finding meaning in structured stylistic devices is not simply a matter of being perceptive and ingenious enough to point out patterns in the text, then moving directly to suggestions about the significance of the patterns. As my countersuggestion shows, the text often will exhibit different patterns, forcing methodological reflection on how we know which patterns are significant. In this reflection Lohfink has not gone very far. He does make some appeal to the principle of intentionality. Structure is not accidental but wherever it is found, it is a token of an intentional consciousness behind it. Structure does not just happen. Consequently, whenever one finds structural devices, one may conclude that it is intentional and therefore significant.

This assumption is, of course, plausible. If we find a line of stones on a trail which form an arrow, we are more than likely right in assuming that it represents someone's message and not a natural formation. And it is therefore significant. But the assumption does not help at all in the case of a literary work, where the whole text is a human artifact and the issue is not really intentionality—the whole text is presumably intentional—but meaning. There is not to be found within the assumption of intentionality a principle which would decide whether Lohfink's description of the structure of Deuteronomy 30:1-10 is correct or the alternative I suggested. Either would presumably be intentional.

The vulnerability of stylistic analysis to uncertainty and skepticism when only supported by an implicit claim to intentionality results once again from the purely formal nature of the projection of an author/redactor's intentions. No evidence is offered of the author's intentions to create the stylistic device beyond the evidence of the text itself. The argument from the text is circular. It is first assumed that the structure is significant. Significant structure implies a structuring consciousness. The product of consciousness is significant and therefore the structural feature is significant. The weakness of this argument, aside from its circularity, is that it begins with the assumption that the structural feature is significant, precisely the fact that must be demonstrated. It is necessary in the first instance to know that a textual phenomenon is significant before one can assume that it was composed intentionally. It makes precisely no sense to argue that an author intentionally created a structural feature in the text but gave it no meaning or significance. It is an important logical point that knowing a feature is significant precedes the claim that it is intentional.

The plausibility of even the purely formal use of the assumption of intentionality to stand behind stylistic analysis rests on the close relation between intention and significance. If we see an arrow on the path we do naturally assume that because it is meaningful to us — it tells us which way to go so as not to become lost — it is also intentional. Getting the meaning and assuming its intentionality are essentially a single act. The case is very similar with the experience of literature. When we confront a chiasm comprised of verbal parallels or the rhyme scheme of doggerel, in a single step we conclude that they are meaningful and that they are intentional — "Rub-a-dub-dub, three men in a tub" is no accident. This assumption, which functions completely naturally in the process of reading, is far less adequate when forced to bear the logical weight of an argument for the meaningfulness of a structural feature. Then intention is made to look like a causal hypothesis about the origin of the text for which there is no evidence. The weakness of such an unsubstantiated hypothesis is amply demonstrated by the fact that it does nothing to resolve the interpretive uncertainty surrounding Deuteronomy 30:1-10. The hypothesis of intentionality does not tell us whether Deuteronomy 30:1-10 is structured as Lohfink suggested or as I divided it or by some other principle entirely. In stylistic analysis, where the issue is meaning, in the absence of any additional evidence, intentionality is of no interpretive use at all, since in any controverted passage, either side or all sides may claim it equally for their interpretations. Logically, meaning precedes intentionality, which is a deduction from it, although, as I stressed earlier, in the logic of simple reading, the two may be simultaneous, with neither strictly a deduction from the other.

The vulnerability of stylistic analysis, then, does not lie in an inability to locate or suggest meaning for stylistic devices, but in the separate area of proving that the stylistic phenomenon detected is actually significant and that the meaning suggested for the feature is correct. What is at issue is validation of meaning. Lohfink assumes that the vulnerability of stylistic analysis is reduced by appeal to an independent external reality, the author's consciousness, which stands behind some meanings suggested by readers but not behind others and, therefore, serves as a standard for judging validity. But the arguments just presented show quite clearly that the purely formal hypothesis of the author's intentions or consciousness for which there is no evidence but the text itself cannot serve to validate a particular reading. To serve as validation, intentions would have to be known prior to or independent of the act of reading. Then the meaning derived in the reading could be compared to the author's intentions, known independently, and correspondence would constitute a valid reading. But unless the author's intentions are known independently, it is impossible to demonstrate a correspondence, and the principle of validation is lost. The weak reed of correspondence to author's intentions is responsible for much of the skepticism which greets Lohfink's specific suggestions.

The second characteristic of vulnerability involves the historical argument. It is clearly illustrated in Lohfink's treatment of the relation of Deuteronomy 29-32 to the covenant formulary. Klaus Baltzer originally suggested that Deuteronomy 29-30 exhibited elements of the "Bundesformular."[22] Baltzer's purpose was restricted to demonstrating the presence of elements of the *Gattung* in the Deuteronomy text, and in this Lohfink feels he succeeded. But more precise consideration of the text reveals the obvious. Deuteronomy 29-30 is not itself a treaty document. It has a much more complex structure than the treaties, with elements not found in the treaties, a marked difference in tone, a more personal, rhetorical style. The parallels to treaties, though undisputed, are at a fairly high level of abstraction and are balanced by divergences from treaty form. The fit between the text and its extrabiblical parallels is imperfect. Lohfink explicitly recognizes the discrepancy and seeks to account for it by the hypothesis I mentioned earlier.[23] The final form of the text does not mirror the treaty form directly but rather a covenant ritual practiced in the cult which drew its form and conceptual world from the treaties. The similarities to treaty form result from the covenant ceremony use of treaties as a formal mode. The differences arise from the characteristic requirements of the cultic celebration. The modifications are an adaptation to a different social setting.

Faced with an imperfect fit between text and *Bundesformular*, Lohfink is led to posit a cultic ceremony as "the most reasonable explanation" of the form of Deuteronomy 29:1-20, 30:1-20 (other parts of the chapter are later).[24] This hypothesis is not *prima facie* unreasonable,

---

22 Klaus Baltzer, *The Covenant Formulary* (Philadelphia: Fortress Press, 1971), pp. 34-36.

23 Lohfink, "Bundesschluss," p. 40.

24 Ibid., p. 44.

but it is important to realize that Lohfink's cultic ceremony is purely a projection from the text. It is a hypothesis based squarely on the central form critical hypothesis that fixed formal relationships are established by actual practice in a determinate *Sitz im Leben*. Formal structure implies a *Sitz* where it was formed with the hammer of actual use. There is no independent evidence that such a cultic ceremony ever actually took place. No other biblical texts exhibit quite the same form. No liturgies of covenant ceremonies of Israel's neighbor have been unearthed. The argument is highly vulnerable because of the lack of supporting evidence.

Again we need to be clear about the nature of the vulnerability. The structural description of the text is not directly in question, nor even for the moment its characterization as sermonic, rhetorical, ceremonial, or cultic. These may stand on their own as observations about the nature of the text or descriptions of it. What is uncertain is the actuality of the ceremony posited as an explanation of the character of the text. At stake is not so much the meaning of the text which might revolve around the structure or tone of the passage, but the critic's need to account for that meaning by reference to a historical reality, the need to objectify the meaning in order to validate it. The vulnerability is only a matter of serious concern if one thinks, as most critics do, that the acceptance of the meaning of the text is dependent on the demonstration of an objective base for the meaning located outside the text. This demand for an objective base is a constant of critical scholarship and is deemed to be an indispensable precondition of scientific explication. Critics may disagree on just what lies behind the text — a historical event, or a sociological setting, or an individual creative personality — but there is fundamental agreement that there must be something that critics can study independently of one another using recognized scholarly procedures, if they are to hope to arrive at convincing and valid results. It is just this aspect of the critical tradition, the demand for verification, that Lohfink feels cannot be rejected in the modern age. There is no going back. But the critical demand gives priority to the question of validation over meaning and specifies very narrowly the type of validation acceptable — reference to objective forces behind the text. On the other side, Lohfink affirms that the meaning of the text, the assertion of the text, is the primary concern of the exegete. This seems to imply that meaning has priority over validation and, in actual practice, it has appeared that Lohfink begins his considerations with the meaning of the passage. But once he has treated the meaning of the passage, Lohfink feels compelled to objectify it and in the case of both his stylistic and formal analysis, the result has been to introduce a substantial area of vulnerability into his interpretation of the meaning of the text.

In the article that opened this discussion, Lohfink recognized very clearly that the doctrine of inspiration and proper exegetical practice in the theological use of Scripture were tightly intertwined. The acceptance of critical methods which to Lohfink were self-evident had been impeded by an ossified doctrine of inspiration. Lohfink himself makes a major contribution to explaining why the traditional conception of inspiration and the notion of inerrancy based on it will not do in the critical age. But simply detailing the inadequacy of earlier formulations is only a preliminary, largely negative, task. The complex problem remains of developing a concept of inspiration which is at once critically defensible and true to the essence of traditional teaching. And this conception of inspiration can be no mere theory. It must carry with it specific implications for exegetical method so that concrete exegesis based on it is itself critically defensible in method and results yet, insofar as possible, compatible with traditional belief. Lohfink's contribution is in the way he seeks to do justice to these complex, often competing demands. The changes historical critical research has wrought in the doctrine of inspiration are profound. In his article, "Über die Irrtumslosigkeit und die Einheit der Schrift,"[25] Lohfink shows dramatically what unwanted and unforeseen transformations occur in the concept of inspiration when old formulations from the precritical age are joined to the new knowledge offered by critical research. Traditional formulations centered largely, although not exclusively, on the author as the channel of inspiration. Behind these formulations was a simple concept of biblical authorship which Christians had taken over from Jewish tradition. Each book had an individual author, working under God's inspiration, responsible for its content. Within this conceptual framework it made little difference whether one spoke of the inspired author or the inspired work; it came to the same thing. In turn, the inerrancy of the whole book as an entity

---

25 Norbert Lohfink, "Über die Irrtumslosigkeit und die Einheit der Schrift," *Stimmen der Zeit* 174/9 (1964), pp. 161-181.

was guaranteed by its inspiration and its unity was a direct function of its unitary authorship.

Critical research changed the underlying understanding of authorship from single inspired hagiographer to a multiplicity of largely anonymous contributors. Catholic scholars recognized that critical research reduced the role of individuals whom tradition held to be the locus of inspiration and thus directly challenged the inspiration and authority of Scripture. They therefore opposed critical research well into this century. Ultimately, critical methods could not be denied and multiple authorship was recognized. What was not clear at the time was the full implication of accepting the multiplicity of authorship while retaining the traditional focus on the author as the locus of inspiration. Lohfink makes those implications clear and they are very disturbing when fully recognized. First, it was no longer possible to speak of a whole book's being inspired in the same sense as formerly. The contribution of each author or redactor was uniquely inspired in itself, even if it were only a snippet. The unity of the whole was left without a principle to justify it. This in itself was a departure from tradition, which had never maintained the inspiration of units below the level of the book. And it certainly carried with it implications for the reading of now fragmented rather than unitary books.

Perhaps the most distressing implication of the unaltered locus of inspiration in multiple authors is the authority that now pertains to each author's or redactor's contribution. Because each author or redactor is now considered under categories originally fitted to individual authors of whole books, the individual assertions of each author or redactor take on the full authority originally associated with whole books. Each assertion is inspired and infallible. As Lohfink puts it, historical critical research becomes "an inner moment of dogmatic theology."[26] Each assertion must be treated as an inspired article of faith. There is no buffer between the surface assertions of the text and its binding authority as direct revelation. This is a truly astonishing conclusion to Catholic scholars' checkered history with historical criticism.[27] Lohfink suggests two possible ways to preserve the tradi-

---

26 Ibid., p. 165.
27 Ibid.

tional conception of inspiration with its center on the author without the unwanted implications. First, it would be possible to designate the final person to add to the text as its author for the purposes of the definition of inspiration. This would preserve the unity of the book by making it a function of that last "author's" inspiration. The last author's work would subsume all the work of those who preceded him. And inerrancy could then be applied to the final work as in the earlier conception of inspiration. But this exit from the problem leads to rather ridiculous conclusions. The prophet Ezekiel, in this scheme, would not be inspired nor would his most immediate disciples. The last redactor, who perhaps added no more than half a verse, would be credited with the infallible charism of inspiration. This solution will not do.

The second suggestion is to consider every individual who made a contribution to the book as inspired. But each act of inspiration was directed toward the production of the final book, not toward the immediate situation in which the author found himself.

> [O]ne should regard everyone who made a real contribution to the wording and sense of a book as infallibly led by God with reference to the coming book, that is, as inspired. Then with regard to a book that came into being gradually, one must speak of a number of inspired authors. The inspiration of these authors was not directed to their immediate work taken in itself, but to this work insofar as it was ordered by God toward the final wording and sense of the biblical book. As a result the inerrancy which follows from inspiration should not be placed immediately on all the collaborators and their intentions but on the book produced at the end. The inspiration of the many collaborators on a book would therefore be regarded as a whole whose effect of inerrancy is only produced at one point: in the final result of the collaboration.[28]

Inspiration is located in the final result. Within this long quotation Lohfink relocates inspiration from the author to the book. This is really not a radical break with tradition, Lohfink argues, but rather stands in continuity with the sense of tradition. Because the earlier formulations reckoned with single authors, they actually posited the concomitants of inspiration, inerrancy and unity, as attributes of the book. Maintaining the formulations of inspiration centered on the author, while introducing a radically altered concept of authorship twisted the earlier affirmations beyond recognition and led to very unfortunate con-

---

28 Ibid., p. 166.

clusions concerning unity and authority. Reformulations of the doctrine of inspiration which center on the book actually preserve the traditional sense.

The question next arises whether, in trying to remain faithful to the traditional understanding of inspiration, it is proper to speak of inspired books or of the inspired Bible. It must be said that the conception of book lying behind the formulation involving inspiration of each book is decidedly modern. If a modern scholar buys a bookcase and begins to fill it book by book, each addition adds nothing to the sense of the books which preceded it onto the shelf, nor does the accident of their specific arrangement.[29] The sense of each book is an inalterable quantity at publication.

This illustration represents the modern understanding of a book but it is hardly appropriate to the biblical books. In fact, each addition does alter the sense of what had already been written. Within individual books it is clear how redactional touches have redirected the sense, often deepened or completely modified it. Less obvious but no less real is the process by which late additions to one book changed the sense of passages in other books, or indeed the simple combination of the books into a larger unit created new dimensions of meaning. The late additions to Deuteronomy made in the spirit of prophecy compel the reading of the whole Pentateuch in the light of prophecy.[30] Or the inclusion of the Chronicles in the Bible forces a reinterpretation of the narrative in the deuteronomistic history covering the same periods and often the same events. Indeed, each addition involves a change in the meaning of the whole, because, as Lohfink argues, the Bible constitutes a closed system in which each element gains its meaning from the pattern of relations it establishes with other elements in the system.[31] Each addition alters the configuration of the system and therefore the pattern of relationships within it.

The process of adding meaning must finally have an end, and for the Bible, this end came definitively with the appropriation of the Old Testament by the New. To allow for the fact that the New Testament itself was not complete when the Old Testament was appropriated, Lohfink

---

29 Ibid., p. 168.
30 Ibid., p. 170.
31 Ibid., p. 173.

holds that the Old Testament books were joined directly with the New Testament reality, namely Christ. This seems a questionable formulation, given the literary categories Lohfink had been using, but it does serve to emphasize the preeminent effect of combining the Old Testament with the New. Henceforth, the Old Testament was to be read christologically, as part of a larger work whose center was Christ. The final alteration of meaning of the Old Testament text is not on the order of a few nuances added by redactional touches, but is a fundamental new infusion of meaning created by reading the Old Testament in relation to its continuation in Christ.

This last decisive act in the process of composition completed the book toward which all the intermediate steps of inspiration were moving. The full Bible is the telos both of the redactional process and the inspiration which guided it. Only the final book, the complete Bible with its pervasive christological orientation, is inspired in a full sense. It alone constitutes a book in the closed and unified sense posited by the traditional doctrine of inspiration. In the precritical formulation of that doctrine, the book was composed by a single author. Critical scholarship made this formulation untenable. Lohfink in effect substituted the redactional process and, in particular, its decisive last stage for the single author in the traditional formulation. In place of the single author which critical scholarship could not confirm, Lohfink placed an analog which could be supported critically.

Although the redactional process can be made to take the place of the single author in the doctrine of inspiration, it is not identical and its substitution occasions alterations in the extensive system which was centered on inspiration but involved as well the unity of Scripture, its inerrancy and, still further, general rules of hermeneutics and literature. One major alteration is to downplay the role of the author. It is the process that matters, not the individuals involved in the process. The shift in emphasis away from the author accompanies the recognition that many of the individuals involved in the process were not renowned heroes of faith of theological interest in their own right, but shadowy, even completely anonymous figures, less likely centers for a doctrine of inspiration.[32]

The eclipse of the author as the focus of inspiration also leads to a greater emphasis on the work itself. Inspiration, it is true, is not denied to each of the authors and redactors, but it is an intermediate, limited inspiration, restricted to that which contributes to the sense of the final book. It is the result of the composition process, not the process itself, which is central.

The new emphasis on the work brings in train a different construal of meaning. When the author stood in the center of the system, meaning was construed as a function of the author's intentions. Moving the work to the center occasioned a different understanding of meaning. Lohfink signalled the change quite clearly:

> If it is valid on general philosophical and gnoseological principles that the sense of an assertion can never be established without regard to the entire system of relations in which the assertion stands, then in the area of Christian Scripture, this system of relations is always the whole of Scripture — and indeed it is meant so by Scripture itself.[33]

Intention here has receded into the background, replaced by the pattern of relationships established by a particular assertion with all other assertions within the system of which it is a part. This is precisely the assumption made by intrinsic modes of literary criticism. What needs to be noted here is that there is a perfectly consistent and logical relationship between the adoption of this important principle of intrinsic criticism and the recession of the author into the background. Lohfink follows through to its hermeneutical conclusions the logic of the displacement of the author initiated on the critical side by the reduction of the status of authorship by multiplying the number of authors, reducing each one's contribution, and breaking the identification of authorship with the authoritative heroes of faith and on the theologi-

---

32 Denying authorship to venerated figures such as David and Moses does not diminish their stature or reduce them as models of faith and piety. But it does remove that veneration from entanglement in the properly literary question of authorship and the hermeneutical issue of the role of authorship in determining meaning.

33 Lohfink, "Irrtumslosigkeit," p. 173.

cal side by the difficulty in maintaining the unity and inerrancy of Scripture in the face of multiple authorship. Replacement of the author by the work at the center of the system leads naturally to a hermeneutic based on the work rather than the author.

Lohfink's understanding of meaning as a function of the pattern of relations within a closed system forces a reappraisal of the literal sense. The usual definition of the literal sense identifies it as the sense intended by the author, usually understood as the original author, not later redactors. Recreating the author's intentions is aided by historical research of all types. Lohfink's discussion of the multiplicity of authorship makes it clear that this understanding of the literal sense is not tenable if one wants to maintain that the unity of the Bible is at the level of the literal sense and that inspiration and its derivative, inerrancy, apply to the literal sense. Lohfink faces the issue squarely and does not seek merely to make room within the author-centered definition, but challenges the definition. Drawing support from Thomas Aquinas, Lohfink argues, "the 'theological' literal sense means throughout the sense of Scripture read as a whole and in the *anlogia* (sic) *fidei*."[34] The literal sense is the meaning construed internally within the closed system which Scripture constitutes. It need hardly be said that given this definition there is no need for the concept of a *sensus plenior*. Most of the meaning which exceeds the intentions of the original author and must therefore be considered a fuller sense in a system in which the original author's intentions define the literal sense would be included in the literal sense in Lohfink's definition based on the concept of a closed literary system.

As we have seen, Lohfink does retain a strong interest in the author or, more accurately, the redactor. But he retains the author or redactor not so much for the sake of the meaning, but to provide a critically verifiable principle justifying the treatment of the whole Bible as a closed system within which meaning is established. It was the intention of the last stage of the redaction, the stage at which the New Testament appropriated the Old, that the whole Bible be read as a christological unity. Earlier redactional stages had likewise tended toward ever greater unity, although the last stage was decisive. The direction of the

34 Ibid., p. 175.

redaction justifies reading the Bible holistically, and it does so without any appeal to transcendent principles such as the overarching authorship of God. The unity of Scripture is rooted in the same external literary principle as a novel by a modern writer, the intention of the author. The only difference is that due to the nature of the Bible's composition, it is more appropriate to speak of the intentions of the redactors.

The unity of the Bible which the final redactor's decision justifies and the location of inspiration in the final form of the Bible are plainly very closely related. The relationship is an attempt to bring together a critical principle and a theological principle. The third element in Lohfink's considerations, inerrancy, fits squarely within the same frame. Inspiration and the unity of the Bible define the level at which it is appropriate to speak of inerrancy. The key here is Lohfink's hermeneutical discussion. Every assertion derives its meaning from the system of relationships of which it is a part. A particular passage now in the Bible may have originated in a particular situation in Israel's life. We may think of one of the ancestral legends told at tribal gatherings. In that situation the legend established a pattern of relationships only within itself and with the particular circumstances of its telling. And its meaning was consequently defined only by those relationships. That stage of the legend's history, however, was only inspired to the extent it looked forward to the final form of the text, the *telos* toward which the process moved. If a present-day scholar were fully successful in reconstructing that original pattern of relationship and hence the original meaning, it would not be fully inspired and consequently would not be inerrant. When the legend was incorporated into J, it contracted new patterns of relationships, acquired new meaning. But again, this level of meaning was not in itself completely inspired and was not inerrant. Only when the legend reached its final context in relation to all other passages of Scripture could the meaning produced be considered fully inspired and therefore inerrant: "biblical inerrancy can only be posited for the sense established in this way."[35] The advantages of positing inerrancy only of the meaning established by the final text are obvious. Not every factual assertion of the text need be defended to the

---

35 Ibid., p. 173.

death. The "fact" involved may not enter into a meaningful pattern of relations with other texts. Nor must every notion held by J, for instance, be accepted as an article of faith. Lohfink's conception would apply inerrancy, however, to the christological understanding of the Old Testament, precisely the area where the title makes sense and where Christians would properly want to apply it, at the center of faith. Lohfink's formulation avoids a great deal of nonsense while preserving what is fundamental in the notion of inerrancy.

Lohfink's interest in his article, "Über die Irrtumslosigkeit und die Einheit der Schrift," was to adjust the related concepts of unity, inerrancy, and inspiration to the new realities known from critical scholarship. The positions taken in this article correlate with certain of Lohfink's exegetical assumptions, which it is now my purpose to illustrate. For the moment I will by-pass Lohfink's christological exegesis, which is of great interest, and consider only his more general exegetical practice.

In "Die Abänderung der Theologie der priesterlichen Geschichtswerk im Segen des Heiligkeitsgesetzes: Zu Lev 26, 9. 11-13," an article written for the Karl Elliger *Festschrift*, Lohfink reconsiders a passage Elliger had worked through in detail in his commentary on Leviticus.[36] On metrical grounds and because of certain correspondences in theme and vocabulary Elliger considered Leviticus 26:9, 11-13 as part of the base stratum of the chapter, a unit comprising 26:4, 5a, 6a, 7, 9, 11, 12, (13b). This basic stratum of Leviticus 26 showed marked similarity to the vocabulary of the basic stratum of the whole priestly work, which Elliger termed PG (*priesterliche Grundschicht*). It was to be supposed that the same author composed both. Elliger explains the similarity in vocabulary source critically. Lohfink began with Elliger's observations but offered an entirely different (and characteristic) interpretation. First, Lohfink disputed that Leviticus 26:9, 11-13 shared the same meter as the rest of the passage. In fact, the meter set it apart. The thematic and verbal parallels of vv. 9, 11-13 to the rest

---

36 Norbert Lohfink, "Die Abänderung der Theologie der priesterlichen Geschichtswerk im Segen des Heiligkeitsgesetzes Zu Lev 26, 9.11-13," in *Wort und Geschichte: Festschrift Karl Elliger zum 70 Geburtstag*, ed. Hartmut Gese and Hans Peter Rüger, AOAT 18 (Kevelaer: Butzon and Bercker, 1973), pp. 107-113.

of the chapter were not striking, though the parallels to PG were. In this preliminary argument, Lohfink sought just the opposite result from Elliger: to distinguish Leviticus 26:9, 11-13 from the base stratum of the chapter and identify it as a secondary, redactional strand.

If the verses were redactional, what was their function? What was the redactor's point? Lohfink begins to answer by noting, as Elliger had, the similarity in language between 26:9, 11-13 and PG. But Lohfink offers a radically different explanation for the similarity. Leviticus 26:9, 11-13 exhibits PG vocabulary not beause it is itself a part of PG, as Elliger supposed, but because the redactor of vv. 9, 11-13 sought to cite quite specific passages within PG. Close examination of the language in 26:9, 11-13 and the parallels in PG shows pointed allusions to just three texts: Genesis 17, the promise to Abraham; Exodus 4, the theophany to Moses in which the promise of a covenant is renewed; and Exodus 29:43-46, which picks up on the earlier texts, explaining that, as a result of the covenant, God will dwell in Israel's midst. These are three very important texts in the priestly history. What is the point of their citation in Leviticus 26?

The answer lies in the nature of the content of the three passages and in their specific relation to the context in Leviticus 26. Walther Zimmerli first called attention to P's deemphasis of Sinai and the law in favor of the unconditional promise given to Israel's ancestors.[37] All three of the cited texts are key turning points in that shift of emphasis, all three stress God's unconditional promise. One might think then that Leviticus 26 was citing these texts as a summary of the promise theology. Elliger would then be correct in identifying Leviticus 26:9, 11-13 with PG. But one need only look at the context of 26:9, 11-13, Lohfink argues, to see that something quite different was intended. The citations are placed right in the center of a conditional blessing and curse. The effect of this placement is to make even the promise to Abraham conditional on Israel's faithfulness. The revision which P made in Israel's theology by substituting promise for the law and Sinai was itself revised by the addition of Leviticus 26:9, 11-13, in the direction of

37 Walther Zimmerli, "Sinaibund und Abrahambund, Ein Beitrag zum verständnis der Priesterschrift," *ThZ* 16 (1960), pp. 268-280.

the deuteronomistic theology of history, which made the course of Israel's history dependent on its faithfulness to God.

The issue that divides Lohfink and Elliger is the correct evaluation of the verbal similarities between Leviticus 26:9, 11-13 and PG. Here broader assumptions come to the fore. Elliger, basing his analysis on literary critical assumptions, finds it most probable that the similarities arise from all the texts' belonging to a single source. The significance of the similarities is limited to implications for the compositional history of the texts involved. Lohfink's assumptions are quite different. He is more disposed to see a redactor at work. This disposition bears a clear relation to Lohfink's conception of the redactional tendency of biblical editors, each redactor integrating previously unrelated texts into an ever more comprehensive whole. In this case the redactor has used these few sparse verses to integrate the priestly and deuteronomistic theologies of history.

Lohfink's tendency to find meaning in every relationship between texts is also apparent in this article. Elliger saw the relationship of Leviticus 26:9, 11-13 to PG but on the basis of source critical principles could make little of it interpretively. Lohfink took the same phenomenon in the text, but, using the more flexible redaction critical principle, he made a great deal of the parallels. By his explication, Leviticus 26:9, 11-13 is a turning point in the Pentateuch. What is at work here is a disposition to read the texts as comprising a closed system of meaning in which all relationships between texts are meaningful. Genesis 17, Exodus 4, and Exodus 29, when read in the context of a conditional curse and blessing, assume a different pattern of relations than when they are read alone. The blessing they promise is no longer the assured free gift of God but is conditional on Israel's actions. It is the new pattern of associations that effects this alteration in meaning.

Throughout his argument, Lohfink consistently speaks of the redactor's activity in constructing the allusion to the P texts and thus altering the meaning of the earlier texts. The point of challenging Elliger's metrical analysis was to allow 26:9, 11-13 to be considered an intentional redactional modification of earlier texts. It might be thought that this emphasis on the redactor implies a different hermeneutical system from the notion of a closed system of meaning we have been discussing. Fundamentally, this is not the case, although the redactor is drawn from a system based on intentions. The heart of Lohfink's analysis is the assumption of a closed system of meaning. The complex meaning structure of a gracious promise made conditional on

Israel's faithfulness, with its shifting emphases and ambiguous affirmations, is produced by the pattern of relationships within the text. Introducing the redactor serves only to explain how the pattern of relationships which create the meaning came into being by reference to a factor external to the text. The meaning of the text was first known and then Lohfink attempted to objectify that meaning by referring it to an independent redactional process, a process that could be examined and verified by critical study. Again in this case we can see two different hermeneutical assumptions used to achieve two different goals. The assumption of a closed system of meaning establishes the meaning of the text and redaction critical assumptions are called upon to deliver a critically acceptable validation.

But the introduction of the redactor once again carries with it a vulnerability. Some inkling of that vulnerability already creeps in with the realization that Elliger and Lohfink both used critical methods, yet arrived at radically different interpretations. To get a firm grasp on the nature of the problem, it is necessary to return to those verbal parallels which are the heart of the matter, though only one set of parallels, Leviticus 26 and Exodus 6, will receive attention. Close scrutiny confirms some similarity.

Exodus 6	Leviticus 6
4a haqimotî 'et-berîtî	9b wahaqîmotî 'et-berîtî
'ittam	'ittakem
7a welaqahtî 'etkem lî	12a wehayîtî lakem le'lohîm
le'am	
7a wehayîtî lakem le'lohîm	12b we'attem tihyû-lî le'am
7b wîda'tem kî 'anî YHWH	13a 'anî YHWH elohêkem 'aser
elohêkem hammôsi' 'etkem	hôse'tî 'etkem me'eres
mittahat siblôt misrayîm	misrayîm mihyot lahem
	'abadîm

There is certainly a literary justification for suggesting a relation between the passages which contributes to the meaning of both. Thematic and verbal parallels are readily apparent. This much is clear. Lohfink, however, goes beyond the literary observation to a very specific hypothesis about the composition of the two passages. The compositional hypothesis, which requires a literary historical reconstruction, involves a different process of demonstration than the simple literary observation and incurs a more stringent standard of verification. Unless we are to fall back on the principle that all meaningful relationships are *prima facie* evidence of the author's intentions, a position

criticized earlier, we must demand additional evidence bearing on the
compositional history of the texts.

In this case there is no additional evidence, only an appeal to the
reader's sense of what constitutes an allusion and an assumption that
the recognition of an allusion as a literary fact entails a redactor who
is making the allusion. But, because of the different standards appropriate to perceiving a literary relationship and demonstrating a
compositional hypothesis, it is possible to affirm that Leviticus 26 al-
ludes to Exodus 6 without concluding that a redactor intended that allusion. Just examinining the passages on the surface, we would notice
that the closest parallels between the two passages involve well-known
formulas, *'anî YHWH elohêkem*, for instance, which though they are
real parallels and could help bind passages together literarily are weak
evidence for the hand of a redactor. On the other side, the greatest
divergences between the passages involve language that is not
stereotyped. Why would a redactor intent on an allusion substitute
me'eres misrayîm mihyot lahem 'abadîm for *mittahat siblôt misrayîm*?
The effect of the substitution could only be to raise uncertainty in the
reader with thorough knowledge of Exodus 6 whether an allusion was
actually intended.

It is important to be precise about conclusions here. The considerations just raised undermine confidence that Lohfink has the redactional history right. But Lohfink's failure to convincingly demonstrate a
redactional relationship between Leviticus 26 and Exodus 6 does not
mean the two cannot be read in conjunction as a legitimate literary
reading. An interpretation of Leviticus 26 close to that of Lohfink could
be maintained simply by noting that language associated with the
promise to the ancestors has been incorporated in a conditional blessing and curse. This is true whether there is a redactional relationship
or not. This interpretation of Leviticus 26 becomes problematic only if
the literary meaning is held to be dependent on successful demonstration of the redactional process. In systems which take the author's or
redactor's intentions as the determinant of meaning, this problem is
certainly unavoidable. Lohfink's own system is something of a hybrid.
Meaning is a function of patterns of literary relationships, an internal
principle. Unlike Elliger, therefore, Lohfink has grounds for seeing
meaning in the relationship between Leviticus 26 and the priestly texts.
But in order to preserve the critical nature of the explication, Lohfink
holds that the patterns are set by a redactor, an external principle. This
second move, which does not have to do with establishing the meaning

of a passage but with making it scientifically demonstrable, introduces the vulnerability we have just seen. Difficulties arise in the area of objective demonstration which, paradoxically, threaten to invalidate the meaning derived from a legitimate literary observation.

In a second article, "Das Siegeslied am Schilfmeer,"[38] Lohfink considers typology, a means of reading Scripture as a unity once common and still enshrined in the liturgy, but in increasing disrepute in the critical atmosphere that dominates modern consciousness. In part, the low repute of typology stems from the fantastic lengths to which early Christians pushed it in search of christological significance in every detail of the Old Testament. We feel a certain superiority over against this crude enthusiasm. More importantly, critical thought has schooled us to locate the meaning of a passage by reference to its historical origins. With its meaning firmly fixed in a historical setting, it is difficult to expand the horizon of a passage hundreds of years forward to include a quite distinct situation within its meaning. The historical distance overwhelms the similarities which are typologized.

The hesitancy of modern believers to accept typology almost on principle presents problems in contemplating liturgy, in which the typological reading of the Old and New Testament together is a vital part. Lohfink recognizes the problem but holds out for the intellectually responsible position. "If it should not be possible to arrive in the neighborhood of liturgical typology by modern exegesis and with its own methods, then we really must give up this typology."[39]

As a test case, Lohfink takes Exodus 15, the Song of the Sea, a text typologized in the Easter night liturgy with the death and resurrection of Christ and in the liturgy for baptism with the passage of the baptized from death to life in Christ. Lohfink's concern is the legitimacy of liturgical typology, but there are implications for our hermeneutical interests which are worth pursuing.

Lohfink formulates the critical demand with particular reference to Exodus 15. "The passion of modern exegesis is the verbal sense

---

38 Norbert Lohfink, "Das Siegeslied am Schilfmeer," in *Das Siegeslied am Schilfmeer: Christliche Auseinandersetzungen mit dem Alten Testament* (Frankfurt: Josef Knecht, 1965), pp. 102-128.

39 Ibid., p. 107.

(*Wortsinn*). We can thus formulate the postulate: If it cannot be demonstrated that the text of the passage through the Red Sea is formulated typologically in itself, then we must refrain from its typological use."[40] In the specific case of Exodus 15, Lohfink feels that the test can be met. The Song is itself a liturgical piece, a hymn sung by two choirs. One choir recounted God's mighty deeds, the other responded with praise and glorification of God's name. Even at this most superficial level of analysis it is clear that the Song is not a historical report bound to a single event, but a complex religious work joining event and praise in such a fashion that neither descriptive term alone is adequate.

The language used in the Song likewise cannot be characterized as matter-of-fact reportage. Lohfink says in regard to v. 10, "Thou didst blow with thy wind, the sea covered them, they sank as lead in the mighty waters," "Water here is no longer the real sea, but a mythical symbol of the underworld, of death, of chaos, of night."[41] Here the literal sense of the text rests at the symbolic level, not completely removed from event, to be sure, but already universalized, open to wider realms of meaning. The literal level is the symbolic level.

Drawing attention to the hymnic nature of the Song and its symbolic language guards against driving the Song into the mold of historical report, in which the verbal sense is bound very closely with the historical event. The text itself looks beyond the immediate event to its universal significance.

Lohfink's preliminary observations on the hymnic, symbolic nature of the Song of the Sea caution against limiting its significance to its relation to a historical event, but the heart of his case for typological reading is the structure of the content of the Song. In vv. 8-10 God causes the waters of the sea to stand as a great wall. Egypt enters the sea and God closes the water over them, gaining the victory. For the purposes of analysis, Lohfink characterizes this section as "passage through threatening danger."[42] It is an odd feature of the text that Israel's passage through the sea is not described, though we might expect a similar account. Instead, the expectation of an account is deferred to a subsequent event, Israel's passage through the lands of hostile neighbors.

40 Ibid., p. 107.
41 Ibid., p. 116.
42 Ibid., p. 123.

As with the Reed Sea, God causes the threatening nations to stand harmlessly on the side, like a wall, as Israel passes through unscathed. The pattern, "passage through threatening danger," is repeated, the expectation created by Egypt's passage into the waters transferred to a seemingly unrelated event. The Song itself treats the crossing of the Sea as a *tupos*. Later texts, Joshua 1 and Second Isaiah, also understand the crossing of the Reed Sea as an archetypical event, model themselves on it and continue the typological usage. The liturgy, in turn, just follows the pattern established in the text itself.

Lohfink succeeds in finding a warrant for typological use within the Song of the Sea itself. For our purposes the most noteworthy aspect of Lohfink's argument is that he proceeds by almost purely literary arguments. This involves a departure from traditional Catholic typology, which always spoke of a typology of the events themselves. Lohfink reorients the definition toward a literary relation involving the verbal sense. This is essential because modern readers demand that historical events be connected by historical forces or events. If historical lines connecting events cannot be traced, there simply is no connection. A typological connection then of necessity must seem forced. Lohfink recognizes correctly that typology is a matter of similarity of meaning or structural pattern and that this is appropriately a literary category, not a historical one. He therefore focuses on the verbal sense of the text, not the event behind it.

Lohfink pursues the literary analysis with great consistency in this case. At the outset there is some historical location of the composition, but it is offhand and does not come into the analysis. The designation of the Song as a hymn is expressed in form-critical terms but the form-critical question which leads away from the text to the *Sitz im Leben* is not raised. The form-critical analysis resolves itself into the question of the literary genre of the Song and heightened attention to its internal structure, two voices responding antiphonally. Most strikingly, Lohfink largely avoids the tradition historical debate which swirls around this chapter. Taking sides in that debate could introduce the sort of vulnerability seen in the previous article, holding the analysis and explication hostage to a historical hypothesis. In this case Lohfink does not strike off down that path. The analysis is almost completely intrinsic—the hymnic character of the Song, its symbolic language, the dominant typological literary structure. Lohfink credits that analysis with arriving at the verbal sense (*Wortsinn*) of the passage.

On balance, too much should not be made of this single article. The absence of theoretical discussion means it cannot be taken as a self-conscious venture into new hermeneutical territory. Lohfink does not attempt to support his explication by historical reconstructions, but neither does he work out the methods and principles warranting valid interpretation within a closed system. Pressed, he would almost certainly fall back on critical, historical argument. The virtue of the article is that it does not confront the choice but simply works out the meaning of the song without looking over its shoulder at the need to justify the interpretation. This, at least, sets matters in the right order. Meaning first, then validation.

In 1966 Lohfink published an article entitled, "Die historische und die christliche Auslegung des Alten Testaments."[43] It was intended as a sequel to "Über die Irrtumslosigkeit," a response to questions the earlier article had stimulated. "Über die Irrtumslosigkeit" had been primarily concerned with inspiration; exegetical practice entered the considerations but was not the focus. Lohfink now returned to consider the same issues from the standpoint of exegesis. Earlier we saw that Lohfink drew a distinction between history proper and exegesis. In this article he draws a further distinction between historical exegesis and Christian exegesis. The distinction may best be illustrated by observing the two types of exegesis at work on the same text. In Matthew 1 an angel appears to Joseph and instructs him not to fear to take Mary as his wife. The child she is to bear was begotten by the Holy Spirit. Then the authorial voice intercedes to explain the significance of this event. "All this took place to fulfill what the Lord had spoken by the prophet: 'Behold a virgin shall conceive and bear a son, and his name shall be called Emmanuel' (which means, God with us)." The Christian exegesis of Isaiah 7:14, the text cited, takes the words of Isaiah directly as a prophecy of Christ. This understanding of the sense of the prophecy as referring to the much later figure of Christ is in profound contrast to the sense understood by modern historical exegesis. The critical scholar specifies quite precisely the situation in which Isaiah delivered the prophecy. In 734 B.C.E. Judah was threatened with in-

---

43 Norbert Lohfink, "Die historische und die christliche Auslegung des Alten Testaments," *Stimmen der Zeit* 178/9 (1966), pp. 98-112.

vasion by its neighbors to the north, Syria and Israel. The young king Ahaz went out to inspect the preparations under way in Jerusalem to withstand siege. As Ahaz was surveying the water supply, Isaiah met him and called on him to trust in God rather than human preparations and, as a token of this trust, to ask for a sign from God. Ahaz refused, and Isaiah responded with the passage cited. The child was the sign Ahaz refused.

The differences between the two types of exegesis are so great that it is difficult to conceive of any categories that would apply to both. The Christian exegesis considers only the relationship of the passage to Christ and finds in it a prophecy of his birth. There is no reference to the original context. The historical exegesis explicates the passage strictly in relation to its original context, detailed as accurately as possible.

The opposition between historical and Christian exegesis places believers in a difficult situation. They must read Scripture as Christians. This requires Christian exegesis. At the same time, Christians are not exempt from the intellectual standards and assumptions of their own age. Intellectual integrity demands the historical point of view which characterizes this age.

The situation demands a concept broad enough to encompass both historical and Christian exegesis. Scholarship had arrived at that concept in the discipline called tradition history (*Überlieferungsgeschichte*). The idea is simple enough. The original historical encounter, Isaiah's encounter with Ahaz, is only one moment in the history of his Immanuel prophecy, viewed now as a tradition. Not much later Isaiah himself wrote the prophecy down, combining the Immanuel prophecy with others in a "testimony." The newly enlarged tradition had a different meaning than the original Immanuel prophecy, more pessimistic about immediate prospects, more eschatological in its hopes. A different historical moment brought with it a different sense of the tradition. Later, disciples of Isaiah expanded the tradition again, adding further eschatological and messianic themes, Isaiah 11:1ff, for example, "There shall come forth a shoot from the stump of Jesse." Again, a new historical moment brings a new sense. Each one of these steps was fully historical; they took place within historical time. Matthew 1 could be considered under exactly this same category as a further stage in the tradition, a new historical moment and a radically different sense. Christian exegesis was subsumed under tradition history.

Immediately a problem arises for the theological use of this principle. The Christian stage of the tradition is only one among many. With respect to their historicality, all are equal. Making Christian exegesis historical seems to cost it its claim to authority.

Lohfink accepts the implication. It is the case that all historical senses are equal. But this means, Lohfink argues, that there is no inherently historical justification for historical scholars' preoccupation with the most original sense of the passage — what Isaiah meant in 734 B.C.E. — to the exclusion of later senses. That preoccupation involves a prejudice imported from outside the historical discipline, which Lohfink calls romantic. In fact, any decision to favor one stage of the tradition history over others involves a prejudgment based on outside principles. For the Christian, that prejudgment is a matter of faith. Christ is the canon which lifts Christian exegesis to authoritative status over all other stages in the tradition.

This seems an utter *tour de force*, both in its simplicity and its resolution of the contradictory forces Lohfink sought to balance: the historicist world view and the demands of a Christian reading. But the simplicity of the resolution, at least, is deceptive. Complex hermeneutical issues lie just below the surface. A quick comparison of the different ways Lohfink went about justifying a Christian exegesis in "Über die Irrtumslosigkeit" and "Die historische und die christliche Auslegung" will push the issues into view. It should be said that much has remained the same between the two articles. Both support the validity and normative status of a holistic reading of the Bible dominated by the New Testament perspective. The difference lies in the mode of justification of a Christian reading. "Über die Irrtumslosigkeit" provided a redaction critical warrant while "Die historische und die christliche Auslegung" relied on tradition historical principles. There is no absolute contradiction between the two methods. The redactors are agents of the developing tradition. But there is a difference in the way Lohfink uses the two methods. Redaction criticism provides a dynamic principle. It is the process of ever more comprehensive redaction leading to the final unification of the whole Bible which justifies a holistic reading of the Bible, a reading seeking and thriving on points of connection. Tradition history, surprisingly, is completely static. It is not the process of developing tradition leading toward the whole Bible which supplies the principle to support the Christian reading. Support is drawn from the fact that the Christian reading, like all the other static points on the tradition historical continuum, is a historical point. The developing line of tradition, itself a dynamic process, is sliced vertically into a series of static points in order to relativize the historicity of each point, including the point representing Christian exegesis.

Why this change to a static model? Part of the answer lies in the difficulty in detailing the historical process of the progressive development of tradition. The biblical texts are spotty in representing traditions. For all we know, the record is completely haphazard. For the crucial period just before the New Testament appropriation of the Old Testament, there are no biblical texts and very few nonbiblical sources directly representing a further development of biblical traditions. For the whole period of the formation of the biblical tradition there is very little information, internal to the Bible or external, which bears on the individuals or forces shaping the tradition. Information of this order is essential if one is to chronicle the historical process of the formation and development of tradition and not just the results of that process, particular literary texts.

Part of the answer is also that most of the process of tradition formation does not have the Christian theological dimension that is Lohfink's central interest. The early disciples of Isaiah had no thought of a unified Old and New Testament and only very narrow nationalistic hopes of a Davidic Messiah. In advancing the messianic tradition they did not anticipate Christ. To focus on the whole tradition-forming process would detract from Lohfink's theological conclusions, which are based on the results of the very last stage of tradition formation. The last stage alone is theologically normative. Earlier stages do not really matter theologically.

Another aspect of the answer is that the process of tradition formation is often an embarrassment to a critically trained reader. Matthew's use of Isaiah 7 rests on an earlier, imprecise translation of the Hebrew word 'almâ, "young woman," as Greek parthenos, "virgin." Matthew's own contribution when examined with a critical eye amounts to proof-texting, pulling part of a verse out of context. The tradition, where we are able to see the concrete steps by which it advanced, progressed naturally but often in ways we would not now recognize as legitimate. The problematic nature of the process can then impugn the results, the

Christian readings. Lohfink is aware of the problem and attempts to meet it by distinguishing between the actual techniques used to form a new stage in the tradition and the motives or principles behind them. "It is a matter of the principle, not the concrete technique of exegesis."[44] This really will not do if one is working with the process of tradition formation, the historical question.

The heart of the matter is that Lohfink is not concerned with a historical process at all. His concern is only with the result of that historical process, the conjunction of the Old Testament with the New and the christological reading of the whole that results. To return to our example, Lohfink is concerned to read Matthew 1 in the particular relation to Isaiah 7 that it itself intends, namely, prophecy and fulfillment. Lohfink is seeking an external warrant for the natural reading of the passage and in this search the effect of the development of tradition serves his purposes, while the historical process of tradition formation does not. The reference to history, the suggestion that Matthew 1 and Isaiah 7 are somehow historically related, is only made to keep the discussion, however formally, within the bounds of the historicist world view.

But the process nature of tradition history cannot be factored out to leave only the pure textual relationship between Matthew 1 and Isaiah 7. To say that Matthew 1 and Isaiah 7 both were composed in a historical moment is self-evident and is not yet a historical observation. Even to say that both are points on the same historical continuum, the messianic tradition, is only to designate the area of research, not to posit any concrete historical relation between the two. The historical relation must be demonstrated, then specified and characterized. Lohfink simply is not operating historically when he says that what matters in the first instance is the principle, not the concrete techniques by which the tradition advanced.

It is, in fact, noteworthy how little appeal is made to concrete historical research. Lohfink makes no effort to connect Matthew 1 to the immediately preceding stage in the tradition, its most proximate historical connection. Nor does he exhibit any interest in the tradents or the forces shaping the tradition. Why is that the case? If one looks even

---

44 Ibid., p. 105.

superficially at Matthew 1, it is clear that the passage is not related to some putative late stage in the messianic tradition out of which it grows by historically describable processes, but directly to Isaiah 7:14. Matthew 1 leaps over the tradition and makes a direct literary connection with Isaiah 7:14. This is most often the case in "Christian exegesis." The case is even clearer, for instance, in the next citation in Matthew 2, the citation of Jeremiah 31, "Rachel weeping for her children." So far as we know, there is no intermediate stage in the tradition joining Jeremiah 31:15 and Matthew 2:18. The relation is purely literary and not historical at all.

If one insists on disregarding the literary nature of the relation of the texts and in fact attempts to read Matthew 1 against its tradition history, misinterpretation results. Then Matthew 1:23 must be read as incorporating the entire burden of the messianic tradition which came before it and the sentence becomes very pregnant indeed. But if one reads Matthew 1 naturally without insisting in advance that the full weight of the messianic tradition be loaded onto it, then the citation of Isaiah 7 appears to have a more narrow focus. Its interest is centrally on the fact that it was prophesied that a virgin would conceive. Mary, a virgin, has conceived. It is this prophecy-fulfillment relation and its miraculous nature that is at the center of interest. Naturally, there are messianic overtones. The very fact of a virgin's conceiving signals the miraculous nature of the birth. The name Immanuel is not neutral, as the narrator makes sure we are aware. Matthew 1 then establishes literary relations with other messianic passages where the name Immanuel appears. Certainly there are messianic overtones, but the pure tone is the prophecy-fulfillment relation. The tradition historical viewpoint threatens to boost the overtones, bringing in more than the text itself. In this case the difference in interpretation is subtle, to be sure, but the tradition historical emphasis still somewhat distorts the sense of the text itself. Lohfink does not engage in this type of tradition historical exegesis, perhaps because of his sense that it diverges from the Christian exegesis of the text represented in the New Testament. The meaning suggested by truly rigorous tradition historical exegesis would not coincide with the meaning in the text. Lohfink would be no further ahead on the problem of validating the Christian reading of the text.

The flaw in Lohfink's argument can be analyzed using the categories of dynamic and static from the earlier discussion. The relationship between Matthew 1 and Isaiah 7 that matters interpretively is essentially static. The two passages are simply juxtaposed, with explicit instructions from the narrator of Matthew 1 how that juxtaposition is to be understood. Their specific meaning derives from their particular character and location in a closed system which includes the narrator's voice. The category Lohfink feels should describe the relationship, history, is essentially dynamic, it explains with forces and processes. That dynamic category simply does not fit. If forced to fit, it would destroy the meaning Lohfink seeks to preserve, the meaning formed within the closed system of the Bible itself. The dynamic element is therefore dropped, leaving an empty formal shell and the honorific title "history" for the approach. It is not, however, history in any recognizable form.

The relationships that exist between texts such as Matthew 1 and Isaiah 7 are literary in nature. They are best described using the static architectonic categories of intrinsic literary criticism. In practice Lohfink recognizes this and consequently attempts to construct a static historical analysis by regarding the two texts as points on a static line. History cannot be described statically and the attempt fails. But the question remains, why mount such a strained attempt at all? What is at stake? Certainly not the meaning. Lohfink has attempted to bend historical method to fit the literary, Christian meaning, not the other way around. What is at stake is the method of validation of the meaning. The legacy of the long "love-hate" relation of Catholic scholars with critical scholarship is a conviction in Lohfink's generation that the validation of the sense of texts, even the strictly literary sense, must be historical. This conviction leads to the imperfect grafting of alien categories onto the established stock of traditional readings. It is a combination which cannot flourish.

Conclusion

Throughout Lohfink's work, commendable attention is paid to the plain meaning of texts. Meaning is the exegete's rightful territory, the area to be explored, charted, and presented to the reader. The object is always clarity on the assertions that the text itself makes.

The close attention to meaning prepares a most important observation. Not all of the assertions of even an ancient text such as the Bible are directly related to history, much less directly dependent on historical information. The texts quite plainly express their sense without demanding that the reader reconstruct any historical situation. The meaning is understood on other grounds.

Taken together, these principles specify the relation between meaning and history. Meaning is the primary category; the question of textual meaning always has priority for the exegete over the question of history. Historical information is instrumental in some texts in specifying the meaning, but historical reconstruction is not an exegetical end in itself. Its application, the intent to which history comes into consideration, is controlled by the meaning of the text. Its relevance is not a presupposition but must be justified by reference to the pattern of meaning in the text. Lohfink's major contribution is to take a clear and strong stand in defining the relation between meaning and historical information, giving natural priority to textual meaning.

Placing meaning at the center of the exegetical system reflects Lohfink's judgment that it is the plain meaning of the text which is theologically significant. This judgment is expressed in terms of inspiration. Only the meaning established by the whole Bible, not any of the constructive phases or formative situations in the composition of the Bible, is fully inspired. It is the meaning and not the process that is inspired. Further, placing meaning at the center allows continuity with the tradition of earlier biblical exegesis stretching back to the New Testament and the founders of the Church. That tradition often did not ground its interpretations in history but in the direct reading of the sense of the Bible read as a whole. Placing meaning at the center tends to restore the integrity of these earlier interpretations; they are defensible exegetically despite their unhistorical character because historicity is not the final arbiter of meaning.

While Lohfink emphasizes literary meaning — I believe because of these theological considerations — he is still a product of his age, a modern, post-*Divino Afflante Spiritu* Catholic scholar, and this means history must be taken very seriously. The importance of historical knowledge is never denied and is, in fact, integrated into Lohfink's emphasis on the meaning of the text. In some cases understanding the meaning of the text is dependent on historical knowledge. In these cases exegesis is, at least in part, a historical enterprise. In practice Lohfink is inclined to locate much of the meaning of texts within their historical background; he is disposed to find much of the text related to history. But in his exegesis, historical information always remains instrumental to determining meaning and never rises to an end in itself.

Lohfink also uses history in a completely different way in his articles, as a validation for principles of interpretation or for particular readings or interpretations of individual texts. The issue here changes from the meaning of the texts to validation of meaning. It is this use of history that raises problems. As we have seen, vulnerabilities and possible misinterpretation are introduced into exegesis by forcing the use of historical categories when literary categories are more appropriate. Relying exclusively on history as the sole form of acceptable validation forces just these problems.

The restriction of the area in which to find acceptable validating principles for exegesis is understandable in the light of the history of Catholic biblical scholarship. After *Divino Afflante Spiritu* ended the long quarrel in favor of historical criticism, critical validation simply was historical. To back up a proposed reading meant to describe the historical circumstances that made the reading probable. What marked one out as a critical scholar was the concern to provide some objective validation for an interpretation. This required historical research. When Lohfink drew the important distinction between history and exegesis, he did not reflect on its implications for how one validates textual meaning that is independent of history, but simply took over the historical methods and categories that prevailed among critical scholars. The result, I believe, is some confusion and distortion. If nothing else, a scholar such as Lohfink is drawn to see more of the meaning of a text as historically determined if the only means of validation available to him are historical. This leads to partial defection from the very central principle that the meaning of the text is paramount and determines if and to what degree historical information is relevant. Lohfink raises in an acute fashion the issue of how one validates a literary reading without providing much assistance in answering it. That question will be taken up in the next chapter.

Chapter 5

Conclusion: Toward a Consistent Literary Model

The complexity of the theological and exegetical problems left unresolved by *Divino Afflante Spiritu* has called forth a diversity of responses. Raymond E. Brown, Luis Alonso-Schökel, and Norbert Lohfink have made different assessments of where the heart of the problem lies. Their programs have been directed accordingly, so that it might seem that the only thing their work has in common is a shared desire to expand the possibilities of exegesis beyond the limits imposed by exclusive use of historical critical methods. But though all three scholars begin at very different points and their differences may not be minimized, they all move in a common direction. Searching for a route around and beyond historical criticism, all three move toward intrinsic literary criticism.

The turn toward intrinsic criticism is most obvious and most highly developed theoretically in the work of Alonso-Schökel, who is quite explicit about substituting a literary model for the historical. The fundamental assumptions of intrinsic criticism are far less obvious in the work of Raymond Brown on *sensus plenior*. Grouping Brown with Alonso-Schökel as an intrinsic critic may turn heads. Certainly as long as Brown remained actively involved in the discussion of the *sensus plenior*, he retained the formulation of that theory which referred meaning to the two authors of Scripture. Authorship as a causal explanation of the text is an extrinsic category. But two things need to be noted. First, the *sensus plenior* is linked to God's consciousness as its cause only in a very formal sense. There is no attempt to demonstrate the connection. Second, in practice Brown increasingly tended to downplay the role of the author. No doubt this was because most of the objections to the theory were directed at the role proposed for the human author. The human author was posited to act in ways without analogy in usual human authorship, while God assumed the normal human role. Brown therefore increasingly came to refer not to the

author, but to what I earlier called the *a posteriori* observation of meaning in the text. His strongest counterargument to objections was simply to invite attention to the observable fact that there was more or
additional meaning when an Old Testament passage was read in conjunction with a New Testament text than when it was read alone. In
practice his attention shifted from putative cause to literary effect, and
this is to enter the ambit of intrinsic criticism, though not, of course, to
step in fully.

The fact is, then, that all three scholars were drawn toward intrinsic
criticism in order to solve the problems of compatibility of modern exegesis with traditional theology and the theological applicability of
Scripture. This is not surprising. Traditional exegesis is far more
literary than historical. Before questions of authorship, literary history,
historical referentiality and so forth intervened, the Bible was read as
a whole, its literary meaning apparent in the reading process. The
referentiality of the text to actual historical events was just assumed
and a requirement to prove that assumption or to bring the text's view
of history into line with history constructed on other grounds was never
demanded. The holistic reading was rooted in the conviction that God
was the author of Scripture. God's authorship was not understood according to strict analogy with human authorship, so that it was transformed into a theory of immediate causation, the extreme to which the
sensus plenior pushed it. God's authorship was not a theory in this sense
at all, but more an affirmation about the nature and authority of Scripture. Ultimately, it constituted an informal rule of reading—the text
was to be read as a whole because it had a single author.

Likewise, the use of Scripture in the liturgy is more literary than historical. The simple act of reading the Scripture lesson in a worship service is more a literary act than an instance of historical investigation or
reflection. When the Old Testament, Epistle, and Gospel lessons are
read together, perhaps with a responsive Psalm, the association of
themes is more likely to be on literary grounds than on historical. Most
liturgical use of Scripture is literary in character.

An intrinsic literary approach seems better able to do justice to the
diversity of genres found in the text. Not everything in the Bible is history, as Lagrange early recognized. To concentrate either on those genres most similar to modern historiography or on those aspects of a text
most explicable in historical categories represents a severe and unwar-
ranted reduction. Restricting meaning to historical information or ex-
plicating meaning only with reference to historical causes artificially

narrows the base for a theological use of Scripture. This restriction squanders the broader meaning apparent through a literary reading, meaning that could be theologically productive.

Going still further, adoption of an intrinsic literary model avoids the very problematic base historical criticism provides theology. In the historical model the relationship between historical situation and textual meaning is, in some sense, cause and effect. The cause is always a historical reconstruction which by its very nature is hypothetical. The effect, the meaning of Scripture, is therefore also always hypothetical and tentative, as is any theological reflection based on it. Some tentativeness is acceptable in theology as a check against dogmatism. But the situation that has developed in historical criticism goes far beyond this necessary check. Very few historical reconstructions of more than the most trivial details have managed to win an enduring consensus among scholars. The absence of consensus on the historical situation has extended to absence of consensus on the meaning of the text which is dependent on that situation. Without even a relatively firm base in the text, theological reflection has been postponed. Too often the postponement is indefinite. Theological reflection is adjourned *sine die*.

In the intrinsic model the givens of the text, its patterns of reflections, are always directly before the reader and do not need to be reconstructed hypothetically. Discussion of the meaning does not have to be postponed pending agreement on external facts. The paralysis too often associated with historical criticism can be avoided.

The advantages of a literary model have drawn all three scholars toward an intrinsic literary model. But none of them has gone the whole way to full and consistent use of intrinsic literary categories. Each retains some of the methodology and underlying assumptions of historical criticism, so that their approaches represent hybrids, in many respects very imperfect hybrids. The mixture of literary and historical categories leads to the sorts of contradictions and misinterpretations seen in the individual studies. These problems amount to profound category mistakes – the application of the logic or methodology appropriate in one area to a different area.

The category mistakes uncovered in the individual studies are not trivial, nor are they unwitting. The scholars had specific and serious reasons for mixing categories. For all three, there is a strong pull from historical criticism that opposes an open break. Catholic scholars of the generation of Brown, Alonso-Schökel, and Lohfink stand within a

tradition of scholarship. *Divino Afflante Spiritu* was a hard-won victory
for Catholic critical scholarship. It would be difficult for the generation of scholars trained in the period of the first flush of Catholic critical activity to turn its back on the new method. *Divino Afflante Spiritu*
also aligned Catholic scholarship with the far longer tradition of
Protestant critical scholarship. Catholic criticism was grafted onto the
deep roots of Protestant tradition, so that turning away from criticism
would have meant rejection of a long tradition of scholarship. And it
needs to be realized that in the period in which these scholars were
trained, respectable biblical scholarship simply was historical criticism.
Other intellectually responsible approaches were not available; the
times called for criticism. There are, then, strong historical reasons why
all three retain historical categories while moving toward literary ones.

In each individual case there also appears to be a particular central
reason for retaining critical categories, some fundamental problem
that the literary model does not address adequately, so that the scholar
draws back to the historical model. In the case of the *sensus plenior*,
this central issue is the determinacy of the text. If the text represents
the revelation of God, it must be determinate, that which God wished
to reveal and that alone. The solution here is to turn meaning into a
thing. Things, the stuff of the real world, do not change but retain their
determinate nature. God's revelation in the text is construed as a thing
so that it too will remain determinate. But if the meaning of Scripture
is a determinate object, then the rigorous, scientific methods and assumptions appropriate to the discovery of objects come into play. The
logic of the investigation of objects involves evidence, verification, concrete analogy, all the rigorous methodological strictures that the rich
theological meaning such as *sensus plenior* cannot meet. By making
meaning fully determinate, this approach ironically binds itself to
methods unable to discover the full meaning.

What led Alonso-Schökel to retain critical categories was the desire
to anchor the text firmly in the external, real world. Behind this desire
is a certain disquietude with the usual equating of literature with fiction. Literature, it is felt, is unreal, the product of imagination. Not far
removed is Plato's judgment that fiction is a lie. To provide a connection between the text and the real world that certifies the seriousness
and relevance of the text, Alonso-Schökel nominated the author. The
author was a historical figure well seated within historical reality. To
the extent that the text reflected his mentality or the mentality of the
nation of which he was a part, it was joined to the natural world and

product of it. The connection to the historical author prevented a gap from opening between the text's world and the real world outside the text.

Lohfink was primarily concerned with the issue of validation, how one could certify that a suggested meaning of a passage actually was the meaning. For Lohfink, the issue of validation resolved itself into a question of proper methodology. Lohfink joined the consensus among post-*Divino Afflante Spiritu* scholars that recognized the methods appropriate for verifying a historical fact as the paradigm for validating meaning. The question whether this mode of validation was appropriate to literary meaning as well did not come up. Validation simply was a matter of historical demonstration.

It must be stressed that the concerns that pushed these scholars to retain historical critical categories are legitimate. Any hermeneutical suggestion must deal with the determinacy of meaning, the relationship of the text to extratextual reality, and the principles of validation for suggested interpretations of the meaning of the text. The issue is not whether these concerns are genuine, but only whether they may be addressed in a consistent way within an intrinsic literary model. The confusion and inconsistency generated by mixing categories provides an impetus for seeking a consistent approach.

The obvious starting point for further consideration is the meaning of a literary text. Literary meaning is a complicated subject. To cut through much theoretical argument, the best line is to return to the individual studies, beginning with the *sensus plenior*. The center and strongest point of Brown's argument, in my judgment, was the *a posteriori* observation that when the Old Testament and the New Testament are read together, new meaning appears. The validity of this observation is, I believe, self-evident. At issue is the proper explanation of that meaning. The explanation Brown advocated in his work on the *sensus plenior*, I hope the study has shown, is inadequate. Reifying the meaning by attributing it to the author's consciousness raises questions faster than it settles them. It is this sort of situation that leads one to abandon theories. In fact, the notion of meaning as a mysterious thing residing within the text should be discarded.

Discarding the untenable theory still leaves the original observation of additional meaning in the text in need of explanation. It is a testimony to the rigor of Brown's thought that he first realized the inadequacy of the scholastic definition of meaning, then modified his thought to provide a better understanding. All three scholars moved toward a view of meaning as a function of the pattern of relations between elements within a closed literary system. But in a recent article in Theology Digest, Brown has developed the idea most fully.[1] To be sure, Brown retains the definition of the literal sense by reference to the author's intentions. As a consequence it seems initially as if no advance has been made. But then, following a line very similar to Lohfink's, Brown posits a different sense produced by the redactor. This, too, is a literal sense, apparently because it is linked to an author's intentions, even if the author is a redactor. But the next stage breaks the link between meaning and intentions. Following the arguments of B. S. Childs, Brown recognizes a different sense, the canonical sense, arising when the independent books are associated in the canon. Intentions are not involved at this point; the new meaning is created by the simple juxtaposition of the texts producing a new pattern of meaningful relationships. With the canonical sense it is possible for the first time to speak of the meaning of the Bible since for the first time the pattern of meaningful relationships encompasses the whole of the Bible.[2]

Brown holds that the canonical sense is not a literal sense because it is not produced by authorial intentions.[3] But it is clear that at this point the distinction does not matter very much. The real issue is meaning. While Brown wants to retain a "preponderant importance to the literal sense," there is really no compelling reason to do so, as there was when the author's intentions fixed a single meaning in the text.[4] The meaning of the text is fluid, no longer a fixed thing.

Even the canonical sense is not the final meaning of the Bible. Once established, the canonical text produces a continuous series of meanings reaching to the present. This unbroken continuum of meanings allows a basic distinction between what the text meant and what it means today. It is the meaning for the present that is important.

A major, even radical hermeneutical development lies just beneath the surface here. Through the stage of the canonical sense there is always an alteration in the configuration of the closed literary system to

---

1 Raymond E. Brown, "The Meaning of the Bible," *Theology Digest* 28 (1980), pp. 305-320.
2 Ibid., p. 311.
3 Ibid.
4 Ibid.

which new meaning can be attributed. New texts are brought into conjunction with the existing system. A redactor joins verses or whole books; the Old Testament and the New Testament become a single corpus.

But after the canonical shape of Scripture is set, there are no more internal alterations in the system. Any change in meaning from this point must involve a factor outside the text. For Brown this factor is the Church, which is continually in dialog with Scripture. The necessary implication is that meaning is not simply a function of the text but is a process of interrelation between the text and its audience. The audience or readership assumes a positive role in the creation of meaning.

This principle is extremely important, although Brown does not develop it theoretically. Brown has a remarkable ability simply to see how the text actually works. There are, however, points of contact with current literary theory which also stress the role of the reader. But before taking up literary theory it is important to note some of the implications of Brown's recent work for our original questions about the determinacy of the text and for the larger issue of the relationship between current exegesis and traditional exegesis. First, Brown recognizes not only the possibility of change in the Bible, but also that change has occurred and continues to occur. The meaning of the biblical text is not one determinate thing.

A second implication is that earlier exegetes, the authors of the New Testament, the Church Fathers, exegetes down to the present age explicated the actual meaning of the text. The meaning affirmed by the Church Fathers, for instance, was certainly not our meaning, but it was still the meaning of the text. There are no grounds for denigrating the exegesis of the past. Tradition represents past exegetes' reflection on the meaning of the Bible, their experience of it, and not false conclusions based on a flawed discovery process.

The implication in Brown's recent article that literary meaning results from a process involving both text and reader aligns him with a growing group of literary theorists. Different theorists have arrived at an emphasis on the reader by separate routes. The starting point could be the study of linguistics or semiotics, phenomenology of reading, or the affective criticism of I. A. Richards or William Empson. But the point of convergence for theorists such as Stanley Fish, Jonathan Culler, Wolfgang Iser, Umberto Eco, and David Bleich is recognition of the importance of the activity of reading in producing the meaning of a text. Among these theorists, Jonathan Culler is perhaps the most accessible and clearest. In the discussion of the role of the reader which follows, I will use categories drawn from Culler's important study, *Structuralist Poetics*, at many points.

As the title suggests, Culler's own starting point was structuralism. The central tenet of structuralism is that the analysis of a literary text (or for that matter, nearly any social phenomenon) can proceed by analogy with the linguistic analysis of a language. The linguistic model followed by structuralists is the synchronic linguistics originated by Ferdinand de Saussure. De Saussure conceived of language as a system of relations between structural elements which could be analyzed by making the pattern of relationships explicit. It is this notion of a describable structured system that has been taken up by structuralists and applied to literature.

The greatest contribution of the structuralists to literary interpretation has been to introduce precision into the description of the structural relations which exist on many levels within a literary text. With reference to the earlier individual studies, structuralism offers categories and strategies to describe the patterns of relationships within a closed literary system which arise, for instance, when the Old Testament and New are brought together. The important point is that structural analysis allows these patterns to be described intrinsically; they do not need to be referred to an author or redactor, a referral that immediately incurs the liability of mixing categories. Structuralism can describe the synchronic relations within a text without moving outside the text.

Structuralism offers precision at the descriptive level but it is of less use when one tries to move from the descriptive to the semantic level, to say what the patterns described mean. Structuralism encounters severe difficulties in providing principles which connect the descriptive categories with meaning.

The problem can be illustrated by recalling the narrow controversy between Alonso-Schökel and Casanowicz over alliteration. The descriptive facts were never in question. A series of *yiqtol* forms would be unmistakable in the text and would certainly comprise a pattern of some sort, possibly in conjunction with other forms. But does that pattern convey meaning? Neither Alonso-Schökel nor Casanowicz provided a way to tell and, Culler would argue, neither does structuralism.

The problem of moving from the descriptive level to the semantic is compounded because the continuing close work of structuralists has shown that virtually any text, even a relatively simple one, exhibits an almost unlimited number of patterns. The text can be cut into patterns from different angles simply by sequentially applying different categories: active verbs versus passive, words beginning with vowels versus words beginning with consonants, dentals versus labials, and on and on. Only the exhaustion of the investigator's resourcefulness calls the process of subdivision to a halt. All the patterns discerned in this way are in the text. And all at least potentially contribute to meaning. But are they meaningful in actual fact? The inability to answer this question is painfully obvious in many structuralist studies.

The problem, as Culler sees it, results from the structuralists' misunderstanding of what they are called upon to explain. Ultimately their concern must be with meaning itself, not just the description of structures in the text. Structuralists have centered their interest on structure perhaps because they believe that all structure is meaningful; there is a strong ideological element within structuralism which resists all restriction of meaning. Despite this, it is an open fact that in actual reading every pattern in the text does not convey meaning. Some structural patterns in a text are subliminal. Or, to turn the situation toward its proper interpretation, no pattern in a text is meaningful until a reader makes it meaningful. In the reading process the reader selects patterns that are meaningful and overlooks or disregards patterns that cannot be integrated with other elements to produce a thematically coherent meaning. The process of selection is complicated yet orderly and systematic. In reading a novel, for instance, the reader may ignore the sound of closing syllables. Yet the same reader may find its rhyme scheme the key to a lyric poem. Any pattern of rhyme in a novel is liable to be considered accidental and meaningless. The same pattern in a poem constitutes an important part of the meaning.

By what principles is it possible to determine that some patterns are meaningful and others not? In the reading process, the reader constantly makes judgments about what is meaningful, so that the principles must be sought in the reader's activity, in the competencies by which the reader makes judgments. Reader competency is a concept drawn from the linguistic analogy. If a researcher in linguistics wants to know if a sentence is grammatically well formed in a particular language, he or she will present it to a native speaker of that language. On the basis of mastery of that language, the native speaker reports if the

sentence is well formed, anomalous but comprehensible, or nonsensi-
cal. In a similar fashion, the reader brings to the encounter with the
structured text a competency at reading which consists of mastery of
the rules, conventions, and procedures of reading. A competent reader
"makes sense" of a text, as our idiom allows us to say, by reading it in
conformity with common rules and conventions. Thus the competent
reader knows to ignore rhyme in most prose forms but to pay close attention to it in poetry.

Mastery of the rules and conventions that govern reading is not
necessarily self-conscious. A reader addressing a text does not have
two books before him, the text itself and a rule book for reading. It is
not a matter of discerning a pattern in the text, then turning to the rule
book to find out what to make of it. The actual process is both more
complex and, as we all realize, more natural. To use Wittgenstein's
famous example, it is like knowing the rules of chess. In chess (or in
reading) we do not constantly refer to formal rules of play. We are not
normally even conscious of them as we play. But the rules are implicit
in correct play. The game could not proceed without them. Further, if
a player makes a false move, they may be cited to correct it. The process
of reading is rule-governed in just the same sense.

Before going on, it is important to return once again to the issue of
determinacy of the text. It should be even clearer now that meaning is
not fully determinate. But it is now possible to say more precisely why
this is the case. Literary meaning involves a text and reader. The text
is fixed, its structure normally unalterable. But the other component,
the reader, or more precisely, the conventions and rules the reader follows, are fluid. The conventions governing reading are not like immutable natural laws, but continually change in response to changes in
the general culture and, more particularly, to changes in the collective
shape of literature as an institution. In this hundredth anniversary year
of the birth of James Joyce, it is appropriate to think of the expansion
of literary competency brought about by Joyce's literary work. *Ulysses*
was virtually incomprehensible when Joyce published it; readers did
not have the competencies necessary to make sense of its jumps and
non sequiturs. But *Ulysses* itself created new competencies. If it is still
a demanding, difficult book, *Ulysses* is now comprehensible according
to conventions it helped fashion. And other literary works, even those
predating *Ulysses*, are now comprehended in a different way because
of conventions established by Joyce's work. Literature itself continually reshapes the conventions of reading.

The conventions are also subject to cultural changes. One need only imagine how differently we think about many works since Freud uncovered the subconscious. I am not thinking here of heavy-handed efforts to psychoanalyze Hamlet, which are no more than attempts to suspend all the conventions of reading in favor of one new rule. There is something of a rule of reading against this reductionism. But the development of psychoanalysis has created the possibility of interpreting elements of the text as revealing hidden levels of a character's motivation. Advances in knowledge and culture create new competencies. Conventions can and do change, and as they change, the meaning of a literary work changes. Meaning is dynamic, so that the text speaks afresh to every generation of readers and in their own language.

Suggesting that meaning changes because of changes in what the reader brings to the text seems once again to throw open the door to exegetical anarchy. Interpretation runs riot, each reader a petty tyrant over the text. In theology, emphasizing the role of the reader in creating meaning seems the Protestant principle raised to the ultimate power.

The issue therefore shifts to validation, the issue that most concerned Lohfink. How is any reading of a text to establish its claim to validity for more than the individual reader? It is not evading the question at all to answer that it depends. It depends, in one dimension, on how the text is being used. If the biblical text is being used as a historical source, for instance, then validation in that use mandates conformity to the canons of historical proof. The biblical source must be compared with other sources. The reliability of the witnesses must be gauged by their proximity to events they report and so forth.

It is a mistake, however, to proceed as if the method appropriate to the historical use of the biblical text were universally applicable or paradigmatic of all validation. It is equally a mistake to think that the degree of certainty obtainable in the physical sciences or even the social sciences provides the standard for all validation, that the literary critic should aim for a single, univocal meaning which is certifiably valid. Lohfink tends toward these mistakes and they compromise his interpretation. Literary critics have been too eager to join the ranks of scientists. Literary meaning in many situations of use does not constitute a determinate object, but a controlled process, so that the methods of validation appropriate to objects do not apply. And it is the nature of most literature to be open to more than one reading—in fact, to resist the demand to yield up one certain, unambiguous meaning.

The mantle of certainty borrowed from the sciences does not fit literature.

The key to the validation of literary meaning is the recognition that the reading process is an orderly, rule-governed procedure. The analogy of reading with chess is again illuminating. The rules of chess do not strictly determine the play; the game is infinitely variable. But the rules do function in individual moves (the player will only move the bishop diagonally) and they identify false moves (if the player moves the bishop up two and to the left one square). Conventions and rules function in a similar way in literature to direct and control the reading process. There is, for instance, a general though usually unstated convention that repetition of a word sends the reader back to the original occurrence to make a meaningful connection. The space between the repeated words can be fairly great. In William Blake's "Holy Thursday," the word "land" occurs in two different stanzas:

> Is this a holy thing to see
> In a rich and fruitful land,
> Babes reduced to misery,
> Fed with cold and usurous hand?
> Is that trembling cry a song?
> Can it be a song of joy?
> And so many children poor?
> It is a land of poverty![5]

The repetition of "land," reinforced by the termination of the repeated question formed in the last line, confronts the natural bounty of "a rich and fruitful land" with the social reality of "a land of poverty" to create a moral judgment.

In Hebrew poetry, as we now read it, there is a general convention that the members of a *parallelismus membronum* are to be taken together to produce a single sense rather than taken singly, each making a separate statement. This is very much a convention or rule of reading.

Likewise, specific rules and conventions govern narrative prose. Allowance must be made for certain genres exceptional in this regard,

---

5   William Blake, "Holy Thursday," in *The Norton Anthology of Literature*, ed. M. H. Abrams, et al., Major Authors Edition (New York: W. W. Norton and Co., 1962), p. 930.

but narratives are normally read sequentially as moving toward a conclusion. Details and scenes take some of their significance from their
contribution to the movement toward the satisfying conclusion of the
story. Chekhov observed that if a gun appears in the first act of a play,
it must go off before the curtain falls. The reader expects it, because of
the teleological nature of reading. The story of Joseph at the end of
Genesis begins with Joseph's transparent dream of his family bowing
before him. The reader does not treat this incident emblematically as
a closed sense unit (though the reader will in part take it as emblematic
of Joseph's character), but orients it toward the end of the story. The
dream gives the story an impulse; it sets up a tension that must be
resolved — will the dream prove true? The resolution of that tension is
one *telos* toward which the story moves. The story cannot end until the
tension is resolved, in the actual case by the multiple ironies of Joseph's
serving his family as they unwittingly bow down to him.

The point here is not to explore every rule and convention of reading. This would require what Culler calls a poetics to study and formal-
ize what competent readers do when they read. The point is only to
establish that reading is a rule-governed operation involving conventions mastered by competent readers. The conventions are not subjective in any pejorative sense. It is possible to make a mistake in reading,
to break a rule. Many of my earlier criticisms of the interpretations offered in the individual studies have been of the order that the scholars
have misapplied a convention appropriate to one type of literature by
using it with literature of another type. Their reasons for this sort of
misapplication were usually not misunderstandings of the actual rules
of reading but were of a completely extraneous nature, the need to tie
the text to the world or validate a particular reading.

It is obvious, I believe, that the concepts of literary competence and
reading conventions do not allow the sort of specificity aimed at in the
sciences. There is no means of placing the literary givens of a text on
one axis, then moving along it until it intersects the appropriate rule to
arrive at the meaning. The reader is continuously and actively involved,
selecting, weighing, and applying conventions in response to the text.

Evaluation of the application and weight of different conventions can vary. In a very famous chapter, Erich Auerbach contrasts the style of a passage from the *Odyssey* of Homer with the sacrifice of Isaac in Genesis 22.[6] In the *Odyssey* the narration tells the reader everything he needs to know. There are no gaps to fill. All elements of the events and of the character of the personae are in the foreground, explicit, as are the judgments the reader is to place on them. Genesis 22 stands in contrast. Everything is implicit, understated, unexpressed. No judgments are supplied to the reader. The very sparseness of the account calls upon the reader to fill in what is not stated. Auerbach calls the style of Genesis 22 mimetic and traces the mimetic style from Genesis 22 through the history of literature. From our perspective, that long tradition establishes a reading convention for such understated texts in which the reader is called upon to supply the judgments and depth which the text does not itself make explicit. In the specific case of Genesis 22 the mimetic convention would provide a warrant for importing Abraham's pathos into the passage, his anguish at the command to sacrifice his only son. That emotion is not described by the text, but the reader can supply it from his own understanding of the emotion appropriate to such a situation.

Genesis 22 can, however, be read according to quite different conventions. If one does not supply Abraham's emotions, the most striking thing about the text is precisely the absence of pathos. The tone of the account is very flat and matter-of-fact. The pace of narration hardly allows time for emotional responses. Abraham no more than receives the fateful command from God than he begins preparations, and within the verse he is on his way. If one does not halt to supply Abraham's emotions, then the interpretive task becomes to integrate the flat tone and fast pace of the action into a thematically coherent interpretation. The requirement to make thematic sense of tone and pace is itself a convention of reading. In Genesis 22, the pace and tone can be integrated with other elements of the story by understanding that the story seeks to emphasize Abraham's instinctive obedience to God rather than his distress. The absence of language describing emotions

---

6　Erich Auerbach, *Mimesis: The Representation of Reality in Western Literature*, trans. Willard R. Trask (Princeton: Princeton University Press, 1968), pp. 3-23.

is not a warrant for the reader to supply the omission. The omission is intentional. The text omits emotions because they are irrelevant or would even interfere with its primary emphasis.

Separating these two readings, the second of which I favor, are substantial differences over the application of conventions of reading to this text. Further discussion of Genesis 22 would therefore center on the conventions and their applicability to the text. It would be possible to argue for the mimetic reading by calling attention to several emotionally charged words. Isaac is called Abraham's only son. This might be a warrant for filling in the emotional background. The very situation may be so emotionally intense that Abraham's anguish cannot be ignored. Against these arguments one could emphasize the immediacy of Abraham's response to God's command. The reader is allowed no time to dwell on the situation. The discussion could continue productively at the general level of conventions and textual warrants for their application.

The application of conventions involves the reader's judgment; judgments will differ and with them the meaning of the text. These differences are at the level of the reader's general competence in reading any text. Beyond this there are considerations which affect the choice of conventions in a systematic way and thus affect meaning. Several are especially important for religious literature.

First, it is necessary to note that the situation of use of Scripture varies. The Bible may be read privately in a manner closely related to the way one reads a novel or book of poetry. In these circumstances the usual conventions of general reading apply most strongly. But when Scripture is used in the liturgy, for instance, the situation brings with it some of its own conventions which enter the production of meaning. For example, liturgical use may provide a warrant for more typological association between Old Testament passages and New than the general conventions would warrant. And the way the liturgy pulls passages from their full literary context and juxtaposes them may involve thematic connections between the passages that would not be warranted if both were read, as normally, with immediate reference to their context. Slightly different conventions apply in different situations. The point to make here is that in specifying the validity of a reading, one must speak of validity within a specific situation of use.

Second, the conventions of reading may vary systematically from community to community. Culler's notion of a poetics envisions a generalized competency shared by all mature readers. This generalized competency does exist and constitutes a common possession of all good readers, but different groups have additional distinctive conventions of their own or predispositions to apply certain general conventions rather than others. This situation is very clear in regard to Scripture. There are systematic differences in reading conventions between Christians and Jews, Catholics and Protestants, liberal denominations and conservative, that amount to special subsets of the general rules of reading. The pattern of use of the conventions assumes a distinct and characteristic shape within these communities. The implication here for the issue of validation is that within each group a particular reading will be judged not by its conformity to the general rules of reading, but by its conformity to the rules observed by that community. This is obvious in the discussion of the meaning of Scripture between readers coming from different traditions. It does not seem, further, that it is possible to establish any one set of universally acceptable conventions so that all traditions in the conventions of reading they use cannot be transcended by a general set of conventions. Nonetheless, understanding the role of reading conventions in producing meaning and the systematic nature of the differences in conventions between traditions may sharpen the perception of where the difference lies in any discussion of particular passages of Scripture involving readers from different backgrounds.

At the end of these considerations it is possible to formulate some general principles about the nature of validation of a literary reading. First, both the determinacy of the structural patterns in the text and the rule-like nature of the conventions governing the reading process construct limits beyond which a reading is idiosyncratic, perverse, or simply wrong. It is not possible under any current conventions to read Genesis 22 as a farce. Different readers can hold rational and productive discussions on the conventions that apply to any passage and the textual warrants for their application. It is possible to change another reader's mind, show a better reading, or understand and profit from another's reading. All these activities imply that there are valid and invalid readings, not just purely subjective responses. On the other hand, there is fluidity in the application of conventions. Reading conventions do not function as natural laws according to the nature of their object, but they are brought into play according to the judgment of the reader. The judgment of the reader may vary because of the natural ambiguity of the rules of reading or because of systematic differences in the situation in which the text is read or in the set of conventions the reader has mastered.

What is absolutely clear, I believe, is that on internal grounds it is not possible to validate a singular reading as the meaning of the text. The assumption that this is the goal of criticism is, in any case, a mistaken transference to literature of standards applicable perhaps only in mathematics and the more mathematically based physical sciences. What may be validated most directly in literature is the process by which meaning is created. The reader either follows the rules of reading or doesn't. The reading is accordingly valid or invalid. But even here it is necessary to recall that the judgment of validity takes place by reference to rules that govern reading in a particular situation of use and are operative for a specified group of readers.

The principles of validation appropriate to literature do not, therefore, certify a single meaning as correct, universal, or inalterable. Literary meaning is fluid. This is a positive attribute, not a debilitation. But if literary principles allow different valid readings, it is also the case that different groups will only consider certain of the possible meanings valid. There is, then, a type of validation that takes place outside the bounds of strictly literary principles. Again, this is particularly true of Scripture. Proposed readings of Scripture are tested against traditional understandings of the same text and against traditional affirmations of faith. And ultimately interpretations of Scripture are judged by their capacity to shape and direct the life of faith of the community to which they are directed. If a reading, however in conformity with the conventions of reading, fails to direct and enrich the life of faith in the community, it will be dropped. The final validation of a literary reading of Scripture lies in the practice of faith it empowers.

This brings us to the last concern, the relation of the text to the outside world. There has always been a tendency to link the meaning of the text as tightly as possible to the outside world, often by using causal explanations in which the cause stands firmly rooted in the objective world. There are several reasons for this. One has to do with validation. Whether the theorist considers it a problem or a blessing, meaning is elusive. It changes, escapes us, submerges, resurfaces. Two equally intelligent people can disagree on it. The theorist can pin the meaning down only by linking it to stable phenomena in the extratextual world. These phenomena can be verified and, so it seems, the meaning dependent on them can be validated. In practice the demand for uniform validation gives rise to all manner of determinisms: the

author's psychology, the historical circumstances of composition, the
Geist of the age, the economic stage of the people, and so on through
many critical programs. The great mischief in these determinisms is
that the meaning of the text is forced to fit the procrustean bed of the
determining forces. The true meaning is truncated because, as René
Wellek observed, in literature the effect is always incommensurate with
the cause.

The second reason the text has been tied so tightly to the outside
world has to do with ontology. I have spoken of literary meaning as a
process, an effect of the act of reading. This rather impressionistic
definition coincides with our experience of literary meaning, but it must
be admitted that it does not offer much of an answer to the question,
what is it really? Meaning is not a fixed, material thing. Consequently
it seems that it is not a real thing and that this glaring deficit must be
made good by attaching the meaning to something that is real and tan-
gible. It is, I believe, this sense that meaning has no reality of its own
that troubled Alonso-Schökel. Causal explanations at least have the
virtue of making up this deficit in literary meaning by making meaning
the effect of a real cause.

I have attempted to show, though I have not argued it explicitly, that
literary meaning is fully real in its own right. The text is real, the reader
is real, and the process of reading is real. It is only if one supposes that
the meaning of the text is an object similar to physical objects that
literary meaning appears deficient. It must be insisted that literary
meaning has its own mode of existence, not derivative of concrete,
physical reality, and not to be unfavorably contrasted with it. The question of the text's relation to the outside world is not properly a question of ontology and cannot be resolved by trying to place the text on
the same ontological plane as the extratextual world.

The relation of the text to the world is more properly a question of
referentiality. Does the text refer to the real world outside it or only to
an imaginary world which it projects? The issue is serious, because if
the text only refers to a world of its own making, then we take it as fiction and tend to regard it with less seriousness. Fiction is not a pejorative term in itself, and modern readers are accustomed to taking fiction
very seriously, but there is still the taint of unreality about a fictional
work. What seems to distinguish nonfiction from fiction is that the
former refers to the real world while the latter refers to a completely
imaginary world. That world may be as remote from the real world as
Alice's Wonderland or Aristophanes' Cloud Cuckoo-Land. To treat

the Bible as a literary work may seem to deny its referential relation to the real, historical world and imply its reference to a "merely" imaginary world. That implication then appears to involve an absurdity because archaeologists daily unearth new artifacts produced by ancient Israel. Israel was certainly a part of the real world. As a result, many scholars refuse to entertain a literary model because of the implications that seeing a literary pattern of meaning in the text makes the biblical world equivalent to a fictional world. Israel was not a fiction, so it is preferable to maintain the basic historical model even though it is clear that the Bible is not history in any recognizable modern sense.

I have been advocating the literary model as most appropriate to the nature of the text. There is room within that model, I believe, for the referentiality of the text, so that the simple equation of literary meaning with fictional world can be broken. It can be affirmed both that the text is referential and that the appropriate category for its meaning is literary.

The starting point for our considerations must be what it means for the text to refer to outside reality. The clearest treatment of referentiality is by P. F. Strawson in a now classic article in *Mind*. The heart of Strawson's thought is the famous dictum: "'referring' is not something an expression does; it is something someone can use an expression to do."[7] This is a radical statement. It seeks to overthrow a whole way of thinking about reference. That way of thinking will seem familiar after the individual studies. According to the theory Strawson overturns, the meaning and reference of a term are essentially equivalent. A term or expression is taken to mean the thing to which it refers. We may recall Coffey's definition: "A concept or term *applies to* or *stands for* an object or class of objects." Accordingly, the meaning of the word "tree" is the bulky leafy object standing before my house. Behind this equation of meaning and reference is a generalization from the simplest form of definition. If a child asks, "What does 'tree' mean?", we will point to a tree and say, "That." It seems in this case that the meaning and referent coincide, with the meaning derivative of the nature of the referent. However well this mode of definition suits terms such as "tree," it does not work as well with terms like "unicorn," "hatred," or

---

7 P. F. Strawson, "On Referring," *Mind* 59 (1950), p. 326.

"the present King of France." In such cases the simple ostensive model becomes grossly misleading because it leads one to think that every meaningful use of a term contains a veiled existential claim that the referent of the term actually exists somewhere to bestow meaning on the term. If a term is meaningful, it is because there is a referent for it.

Now, given this understanding of an inherent and essential relationship between meaning and referent, a sentence like, "The present King of France is living in Paris," appears very puzzling. The sentence is clearly meaningful, yet there is no referent to which the expression, "The present King of France," corresponds. This puzzlement begins to weaken the case for a necessary connection between reference and meaning. The case is weakened still further and the actual relationship begins to emerge if we look at possible situations in which the sentence might be used. For instance, a bewildered, lost-in-the-ages person might accost us and say, "The present King of France is living in Paris." In this situation we would certainly not think that the expression, "The present King of France," makes an existential claim, veiled or otherwise. We would not, therefore, answer, "No, he isn't." The man has not made an existential claim we could deny.

By way of contrast, we may imagine any number of uses of the expression up through the year 1789 when the expression was used meaningfully, referentially, and to make an existential claim. Then it would have been quite appropriate, perhaps, to say, "No, he isn't. He is living in Versailles." The same sentence would have been used in the two different circumstances to two very different effects, once to make an existential claim, once not. The only possible conclusion, Strawson argues, is that referentiality and existential claims are not inherent concomitants of the meaningful use of an expression. To refer and to make existential claims are things that an expression can meaningfully be used to do. In some instances, expressions may be used to refer to something or to make an existential claim. In other circumstances, as in the bewildered person's case, they may not.

The point in rehearsing Strawson's logical arguments at such length is that they break the assumption that every referential use of an expression entails the necessary existence of an objective referent for the expression. This assumption gives logical priority to the objective referents in which meaning originates. Giving priority to the referents is pernicious in the study of literature. It means that interest does not lie in the text itself but beyond the text in the realities to which it refers. One therefore reads through the text to the referents beyond, at cost to the integrity of the meaning of the text. Further, since the objective referents are what really count, because meaning originates with them, any means independent of the text that lead to the referents are valid. The text may be circumvented to get at the reality behind it. If, then, in pursuing the objective referent behind the text it is found that the original text does not correspond to the objective reality to which it appears to refer, there are two alternatives. Either the text is false, and therefore dispensable, or it is fiction, referring to an imaginary world not subject to verification and of uncertain relation to the real world. That is, the meaning of the text is made subject to the verification of its referents.

Strawson's separation on logical grounds of reference from existential claims means that it is not necessary to follow the course just indicated in order to maintain the referentiality of the text. That course finally places the question of verification of the referents squarely in the center of the question of meaning, because textual meaning is derivative of the referents. The nature of the referents must be firmly established in a verifiable manner before the meaning of the expression in the text is known. In Strawson's model both meaning and referentiality are functions of the use made of an expression, not of the referent to which the expression refers.

Strawson recognized that in most situations in which an expression is used referentially, it is informally assumed that the referent exists. But this informal assumption is a quite different matter from the logical necessity of the existence of the referent in order for the expression to be meaningful. If the relation between the expression and referent is essential, the logic of rigorous verification applies. If the existence of the referent is only an assumption, then the full logic of verification is not required.

It may seem we have strayed a long way from the original question of the relation of the text to the extratextual world. Strawson provides a route to return to that question. Strawson's fundamental argument is that expressions assume different logics according to their situation of use. Not every use of an expression is referential; not every referential use of an expression makes a formal existential claim demanding verification.

The question then is, what is the logic appropriate to the use of Scripture? This is a complicated question. What follows constitutes only general reflection on the issue, not an attempt to prescribe "the logic of Scripture." First we should note the obvious. The normal use of

Scripture is to read it. There are other uses: citation in theological argument, use in prayer, and so on, but the most common use is reading. In this situation the reader is not personally using the language directly to make a reference, for instance. Rather, the reader takes the text to be making a reference. The reader makes a judgment about what the text is doing. And, in certain circumstances, the reader makes the informal assumption that the reference the text makes is to an actual object or situation. The assumption is informal in the same sense as earlier noted. The reader does not stop to seek evidence of the relationship or to verify it systematically. The full logic of historical verification does not apply to this informal assumption made in the course of reading. The reader makes the informal assumption that the reference is to the real world only under certain circumstances. It is clear that the assumption is not always made. In the case of parables, for instance, we do not assume that there was an actual prodigal son or an actual Good Samaritan. To specify the circumstances under which the assumption is made, it is necessary to introduce the concept of naturalization, a concept used by Culler. Naturalization is the process of "making sense" of a text by bringing it "within the modes of order which culture makes available, and this is usually done by talking about it in a mode of discourse which culture takes as natural."[8] The text, which initially is somewhat alien and unknown, yields sense by being connected with what the reader already knows. This is a structured, orderly process, again controlled by what the text itself presents and by appropriate conventions. Naturalization is a part of the reading process and subject to its conventional nature.

Culler distinguished five levels or modes of naturalization to which the reader connects the givens of a new text. Two are completely literary: the new text is taken to be parodying a genre with which the reader is familiar, or the language of the new text is taken to be drawing attention to the nature of language itself. Examples of both types of naturalization can be found in the Bible, but neither level is pertinent to the relationship of the text to the outside world, the issue here. The three other modes are, however, very pertinent.

---

8   Jonathan Culler, *Structuralist Poetics* (Ithaca: Cornell University Press, 1975), p. 137.

The first mode of naturalization is what Culler calls the "real":

> This is best defined as a discourse which requires no justification because it seems to derive directly from the structure of the world. We speak of people as having minds and bodies, as thinking, imagining, remembering, feeling pain, loving, hating, etc., and do not have to justify such discourse by adducing philosophical arguments.[9]

This mode is closely related to what I earlier called the assumption of referentiality. The text is taken to be set in the same natural world as the reader. If a ball is thrown into the air, it will come down. If a character commences a trip, he will complete it or break it off prematurely. Concrete details in the text and events progressing according to their self-evident character and natural temporal succession are normally naturalized in this way, so that the text is connected to the real world. Flaubert provides the great modern example of the effect of piling up concrete details until the sense of unrelieved reality becomes oppressive, commonplace, slightly squalid. Flaubert represents an extreme, in which the text is naturalized almost exclusively in the "real" mode to create a particular effect. In the Bible the effect of details is often to strike a contract that what is being narrated takes place in the real world. The itinerary in the first chapter of Deuteronomy, for instance, links the text to the real world by specifying the location of the events at places unknown to the reader but assumed to be in the real world. The text is therefore naturalized as occurring in the natural world but at some temporal and geographical remove from the reader. This naturalization is consistent with what Frei calls the history-like nature of the biblical narrative. In naturalizing the biblical text the reader is aware that some discounting is necessary because the text's real world is at some remove from his own. Nonetheless, the assumption is that the two worlds are coextensive. The text refers to the reader's world, just a different section of it.

The second mode of naturalization involves the cultural understanding of the reader:

> [T]here is a range of cultural stereotypes or accepted knowledge which a work may use but which do not enjoy the same privileged status as elements of the first type, in that the culture itself recognizes them as generalizations.[10]

---

9 Ibid., p. 140.
10 Ibid., p. 141.

When 2 Samuel 11 says, "In the spring of the year, the time when kings go forth to battle, David sent Joab ...," the reader naturalizes this according to cultural expectations of the mischief done by powerful men turned indolent by age or ceremonial responsibility. The reader understands this passage rightly if he expects some intrigue, yet this is nowhere stated explicitly. The cultural mode is not composed of self-evident expectations to the same degree as the real mode. Departures from normal cultural expectation can be accepted within the cultural mode. Not every warrior who fails to go to war falls into mischief, but the pattern is well enough established that we naturalize David's actions as real actions in the real world of culture in which we live. Again the cultural world of David is at some remove from our own — we do not have kings — but it is united with ours by David's conformity to our cultural expectations. The text is history-like in its combination of remoteness and fundamental identity with our world.

The third level of naturalization is that of genre. The reader possesses specific expectations for different genres to which the phenomena in the text can be connected. In fantasies and fairy tales, natural laws may be suspended. The Cheshire cat disappears, all but the smile, in merry defiance of the law of the conservation of mass and energy. In mysteries, seemingly inconsequential details casually dropped early in the story return at the end as the key to "whodunit." The experienced reader of mysteries evaluates and files the least detail as a clue. In such cases, the reader naturalizes the phenomena in the text, violation of natural law or casual detail, by connecting it to expectations of what is natural and normal in that genre, not what is natural or normal in the real world. In the real world, natural laws are not broken and casual details are promptly and properly forgotten.

The importance of this sort of naturalization, which is essentially internal to literature, to our question of the relationship of the text to the outside world is that it helps explain how a contemporary reader processes the nonhistory-like elements of the biblical text. There are many instances of elements within the biblical text which cannot be naturalized at either the real or cultural levels: the division of the Reed Sea, the appearance of God on Sinai, Elijah's translation on the other side of the Jordan. Elements of this type would seem to block the realistic reading of the text and require that the whole text be naturalized on a nonrealistic plane. The concept of genre allows a great deal more subtlety in deciding just how the text is to be naturalized by allowing departures from the usual rules. In mysteries, for instance, most of the details are naturalized as they would be in the real world. But certain details are naturalized not according to the nature of the real world, where they might be ignored, but according to the nature of the genre, in which casual details are taken as clues, red herrings, or traps set for the inexperienced reader. Because of the genre conventions, the reader knows to do something more with details than would be normal in a strictly realistic reading. The reader converts them to thematically significant elements. Something of the sort takes place with regard to nonrealistic elements in biblical literature. The nonrealistic elements in the text first help to establish the genre. Initially they rule out taking the text as strict history. History as a genre does not allow breaches of historical causality. In a text such as the description of the crossing of the Reed Sea, the reader is forced to seek or construct a genre that is at once realistic — the text establishes Moses, Israel, and the Egyptians as real characters — and nonrealistic — water does not mount up into walls. Frei's term "history-like narrative" again seems appropriate to this text. The narrative is like history in that many of its elements are naturalized at the level of the real and cultural expectations of the reader. But it is only history-like because it contains elements that cannot be naturalized at the realistic levels, but must be interpreted thematically as going beyond realistic categories. The miraculous elements in the crossing of the Reed Sea contribute to the theme of the story, God's providential deliverance of His people. Realistic and nonrealistic elements are held together by the genre expectations of the readers, which do not allow one set of categories to drive out the other. Genre expectations prevent the text from being reduced to its purely realistic elements or from being dismissed as fiction because of its nonrealistic elements.

The process of naturalization allows an appropriately literary understanding of the relationship of the textual meaning to the extratextual world by bringing the two together in the process of reading. The reader in effect informally assumes that the text refers to the outside world when he naturalizes the text at the realistic levels of the real and cultural world. That assumption is informal because it is not supported by any sort of external proof. Its confirmation is simply the congruence between the descriptions in the text and the understanding of the real and cultural world the reader brings to the text. That coherence allows the text to be naturalized realistically and the informal assumption of reference to actual realities to be maintained.

If it is not necessary or even appropriate to demonstrate the referentiality of the text by historical investigation, does historical criticism have any role in the literary process of reading, of making sense of the text? Without a doubt. The reader naturalizes the biblical text by bringing it into conjunction with his own understanding of the real and cultural world. Historical research can expand the reader's understanding of the real and cultural world which enters into the process of naturalizing the text.

The additional knowledge the reader brings to the text is especially important because, although the reader naturalizes the text in his own real world, it is in a somewhat remote corner of it. Units of measure are hins and cubits. David flees from Jerusalem, a well-known city, to Gilead, an unknown region. Details of place, terminology, and custom are all somewhat unfamiliar. The reader must seek guidance on how to naturalize them because the unfamiliarity of the details in the text makes them ambiguous. Is Gilead a real place or has David escaped into a mythical region of sanctuary? The reader must make a judgment. In part that judgment will be guided by other realistic elements in the text, so that the one detail, the name "Gilead," will normally be naturalized at the same level as the other details. In this instance the familiarity of Jerusalem would be particularly important. But because of the realistic, history-like character of the text, the reader also assumes that historical information is relevant to settling the ambiguity. Further, the conventions of history-like narrative allow the reader to enrich and fill in the historical background with historical information known independently of the text. Discovering that Gilead was the name of the rugged, mountainous territory to the east of the upper Jordan a safe remove from Jerusalem confirms the reader's realistic reading. But the additional information also enriches the understanding of the passage by allowing the reader to fill in David's motivation for fleeing to this particular region. Gilead is a safe distance from Jerusalem. It is mountainous, making military operations against him difficult and concealment easy. The mountainous terrain is congenial to the sort of guerrilla warfare with which David had built his power earlier. The history-like character of the text and the assumption that the situation referred to is a real situation provides a limited warrant for projecting fully historical information into the reading of the text.

The warrant to project historical information into the text is limited in the same way as every other convention of reading by competition with other conventions and by necessity to integrate any outside information into the pattern of literary relationships already existing within the text. Historical information must be fit into the literary structure so that it does not overwhelm and destroy what is already there. On some occasions there is simply no requirement for precise historical information even in a very history-like passage. For instance, in the Genesis 23 account of Abraham's negotiation for a burial ground for Sarah, the reader understands four hundred shekels of silver as a very substantial price without inquiring into the exact value of a shekel in Abraham's time. In this case, historical information introduced into the reading would be pedantic and a digression. It would detract from the meaning. But in the case of David's flight to Gilead, the geographic information about Gilead can be directly integrated into the reading without any disruption. The text itself seems to raise the question why David fled east instead of some other direction. Answering that question results in a much fuller reading. The difference in the effect of introducing outside information in these two examples indicates that the warrant for projecting historical material into the text is not absolute but, like every convention of reading, is subordinate to the requirements of the whole reading process. Nonetheless, it must be stressed that our recognition that the Bible is an ancient book which refers to an ancient culture and historical context establishes an important convention of reading which allows us to bring the results of our rigorous historical research into the reading process to deepen our reading.

Even though we do assume an essential congruence between the world of the text and the outside world, the relationship is never so close that the two worlds are completely identical. We must be alert to any tendency to reduce the meaning of the text to our preexisting understanding of the real world. The textual world has an integrity of its own that confronts and modifies the reader's understanding of the real world. This is especially true of the Bible. A text such as Isaiah 11 resists consistent naturalization at the realistic level. To be sure, the opening verses are concrete:

> There shall come forth a shoot from the stump of Jesse,
> and a branch shall grow out of his roots.
> And the Spirit of the LORD shall rest upon him,
> the spirit of wisdom and understanding,
> the spirit of counsel and might,
> the spirit of knowledge and the fear of the LORD.

The reference to Jesse, a concrete historical figure, the father of David, localizes the text in the real world. The genre is appropriate to the

praise of an earthly king and the attributes of this expected king are the
ideal attributes of a temporal ruler: wisdom, understanding, and might.
The opening verses are naturalized as applying to a real king. With
verse six, however, the imagery and genre change:

> The wolf shall dwell with the lamb,
> and the leopard shall lie down with the kid,
> and the calf and the lion and the fatling together,
> and a little child shall lead them.

With verse six we confront what Wolfgang Iser calls a blank in the
text.[11] The reader is no longer able to continue at a realistic level, but
must begin to combine categories, fusing the eschatological order of
these last verses with the natural order of the first. The world of meaning projected into the blank is not identical with the realistic world,
though it is not completely separate either. The biblical world is at once
within the real world, yet over against that world, revealing more
profound dimensions of it.

The great attraction of the literary model is precisely that it can com-
prehend the congruence of the biblical world with the everyday world
without reducing the biblical world to the dimensions of the world of
experience. The biblical world is neither fantastic nor mundane. It is
neither limited by what we know of the physical and historical world
nor does it float free of normal human experience. The biblical world
revealed in reading the Bible has its own integrity; this cannot be
stressed too strongly. It is this biblical world that constitutes a fit starting point for theological reflection.

In taking the direct literary meaning as the starting point for
theological reflection, we are returning to the practice of the past. The
theology of Thomas Aquinas, to take the theologian of premier importance in Catholic theology, was based on the direct meaning of the text,
not on what lay behind the text. Both the conventions of reading and
the nature of theological reflection are different today, but the fact that
theological reflection is most productive when it begins with the full
richness of the meaning of the biblical text is unchanged. Paring down
the meaning to critically verifiable dimensions all too often discards

11 Wolfgang Iser, *The Act of Reading* (Baltimore: Johns Hopkins
University Press, 1978), pp. 168-169.

the most theologically significant elements of the text, the aspects of
the biblical world that stand over against our understanding of history
or human causality, that stand in judgment of our common understanding of the world. Criticism brings the biblical world into conformity with the world of everyday experience. In the process its theological
dimension is lost.

Beginning with the full literary meaning does not reduce the tension
between the biblical world and the outside world by collapsing the
biblical world into the world of everyday experience. That would be to
deny the theological significance of the biblical world. The literary
model I have advocated takes just the opposite tack by recognizing the
theologically productive nature of the tension between the biblical
world and the world of common experience and placing the reader at
the center point of the tension. The biblical world and the outside world
intersect and confront one another in the reading process, as the reader
makes sense of the text. The reader brings his understanding of the
world to the reading process and attempts to integrate the biblical text
into it. But in the process the reader strikes blanks, to use Iser's term
once again. The biblical meaning does not fit the reader's model of
everyday experience. The wolf will not dwell with the lamb. But instead
of converting the biblical world into the world of common experience
to resolve the blanks, the reader constructs a broader world of meaning which is able to encompass both the biblical world and the reader's
everyday experience. The confrontation between the reader's prior understanding of the outside world and the biblical world forces him to
reevaluate and expand his earlier understanding of his world and to
see dimensions of the biblical world in his day-to-day experience. The
tension between the biblical world and the reader's world of experience
is resolved by projecting a world that encompasses both, not by denying the integrity of the biblical world.

By refusing to reduce the theological meaning of the biblical text and
by placing the reader directly at the intersection of the biblical world
and the everyday world of experience, the literary model assures its
theological relevance. Confronted by the world of the text in which God
acts and Christ dies and is resurrected for us, the reader must reshape
his understanding of his world. In searching for a model to resolve the
issue of the theological use of Scripture left over by *Divino Afflante
Spiritu*, Raymond E. Brown, Luis Alonso-Schökel, and Norbert Lohfink each sensed the theological power of a literary reading and instinc-
tively turned toward it. But they did not carry through to a fully

consistent hermeneutical model. The immediate aim of this study has been to show that a consistent literary model is possible without ignoring the serious considerations that led each scholar to retain historical categories. But beyond that, the hope has been to show that a fully literary reading allows Scripture to speak directly to its reader, clearly, forcefully, and with its own voice.

Bibliography

Alonso-Schökel, Luis. *Das Alte Testament als literarisches Kunstwerk*. Trans. Karlhermann Bergner. Cologne: J. P. Bachem, 1971.

----------. "Argument d'Ecriture et théologie biblique dans l'enseignement théologique." *Nouvelle revue théologique* 4 (1959), pp. 337-354.

----------. "Erzählkunst im Buche der Richter." *Biblica* 42 (1961), pp. 143-172.

----------. "Hermeneutical Problems of a Literary Study of the Bible." *Vetus Testamentum, Supplements* 28 (1974), pp. 1-15.

----------. "Hermeneutics in the Light of Language and Literature." *Catholic Biblical Quarterly* 25 (1963), pp. 371-386.

----------. *The Inspired Word*. Trans. Francis Martin. New York: Herder and Herder, 1972.

----------. "Sapiential and Covenant Themes in Genesis 2-3." In *Studies in Ancient Israelite Wisdom*. Ed. James Crenshaw. New York: Ktav, 1976, pp. 49-61.

Auerbach, Erich. *Mimesis: The Representation of Reality in Western Literature*. Trans. Willard R. Trask. Princeton: Princeton University Press, 1953.

Baltzer, Klaus. *The Covenant Formulary in Old Testament, Jewish, and Early Christian Writings*. Trans. David E. Green. Philadelphia: Fortress Press, 1961.

Barr, James. *The Semantics of Biblical Language*. London: Oxford University Press, 1961.

Bierberg, Rudolph. "Does Sacred Scripture Have a *Sensus Plenior*?" *Catholic Biblical Quarterly* 10 (1948), pp. 182-195.

Bleich, David. *Subjective Criticism*. Baltimore and London: Johns Hopkins University Press, 1978.

Boman, Thorleif. *Das hebräische Denken im Vergleich mit dem griechischen*. Göttingen: Vandenhoeck and Ruprecht, 1952.

Braun, F.-M. *The Work of Père Lagrange*. Trans. Richard T. A. Murphy. Milwaukee: Bruce Publishing Co., 1963.

Brown, Raymond E. "Hermeneutics." In *The Jerome Biblical Commentary*. Eds. Raymond E. Brown, Joseph P. Fitzmyer, and Roland O. Murphy. Englewood Cliffs: Prentice-Hall, 1968, pp. 605-623.

----------. "The History and Development of the Theory of a *Sensus Plenior.*" *Catholic Biblical Quarterly* 15 (1953), pp. 141- 162.

----------. "The Meaning of the Bible." *Theology Digest* 28 (1980), pp. 305-320.

----------. "The Problems of the *Sensus Plenior.*" *Ephemerides theologicae lovanienses* 43 (1967), pp. 460-469.

----------. "The *Sensus Plenior* in the Last Ten Years." *Catholic Biblical Quarterly* 25 (1963), pp. 262-285.

----------. *The Sensus Plenior of Sacred Scripture*. Baltimore: Saint Mary's University, 1955.

Buzy, Denis. "Un Problème d'herméneutique sacrée: sens plural, plénier et mystique." *L'Année théologique* 5 (1944), pp. 385-408.

Casanowicz, Immanuel. *Paronomasie in the Old Testament*. Boston: Norwood Press, 1894.

Cerfaux, Lucien, ed. *Problèmes et méthode d'exégèse théologique*. Louvain: Desclee de Brouwer, 1950.

Childs, Brevard S. *Biblical Theology in Crisis*. Philadelphia: Westminster Press, 1970.

Collins, Thomas A. and Raymond E. Brown. "Church Pronouncements." In *The Jerome Biblical Commentary*. Eds. Raymond E. Brown, Joseph P. Fitzmyer, and Roland O. Murphy. Englewood Cliffs: Prentice-Hall, 1968, pp. 624-632.

Coppens, Joseph. *Les Harmonies des deux Testaments*. Tournai and Paris: Casterman, 1949.

----------. "Nouvelles réflexions sur les divers sens des Saintes Ecritures." *Nouvelle revue théologique* 74 (1952), pp. 3-20.

Cotter, Anthony J. "The Antecedents of the Encyclical *Providentissimus Deus.*" *Catholic Biblical Quarterly* 5 (1943), pp. 117-124.

Courtade, Gaston. "Les Ecritures ont-elles un sens plénier?" *Recherches de science religieuse* 37 (1950), pp. 481-499.

----------. "Le sens de l'histoire dans l'Ecriture et la classification usuelle de sens scripturaires." *Recherches de science religieuse* 36 (1949), pp. 136-141.

Crenshaw, James. "Method in Determining Wisdom Influence upon 'Historical' Literature." In *Studies in Ancient Israelite Wisdom*. Ed. James Crenshaw. New York: Ktav, 1976, pp. 129-142.

Culler, Jonathan. *Structuralist Poetics: Structuralism, Linguistics and the Study of Literature*. Ithaca: Cornell University Press, 1975.

Eco, Umberto. *The Role of the Reader: Explorations in the Semiotics of Texts*. Bloomington and London: Indiana University Press, 1979.

Enchiridion Symbolorum Definitionum et Declarationum de Rebus Fidei et Morum. Eds. Henry Denzinger and Adolf Schonmetzer. Thirty-third edition. Barcelona: Herder, 1965.

Fernández, Andrés. "Hermeneutica." In *Institutiones Biblicae*. Rome: Pontifical Biblical Institute, 1925. Vol. I.

Frei, Hans. *The Eclipse of Biblical Narrative: A Study in Eighteenth and Nineteenth Century Hermeneutics*. New Haven and London: Yale University Press, 1974.

Gribomont, Jean. "Le Lien des deux testaments selon la théologie de S. Thomas." *Ephemerides théologicae lovaniensis* 22 (1946), pp. 70-89.

----------. "Sens plénier, sens typique et sens littéral." In *Problèmes et méthode d'exégèse théologique*. Louvain: Desclee de Brouwer, 1950, pp. 21-31.

Hummelauer, Franz von. *Exegetisches zur Inspirationsfrage*. Freiberg: Herder, 1904.

Iser, Wolfgang. *The Act of Reading: A Theory of Aesthetic Response*. Baltimore and London: The Johns Hopkins University Press, 1978.

----------. *Der implizite Leser: Kommunikationsformen des Romans von Bunyan bis Beckett*. Munich: Wilhelm Fink, 1972.

Kainz, Friedrich. *Psychologie der Sprache*. Second edition, 2 vols. Stuttgart: Enke, 1954.

Kleinert, Paul. *Das Deuteronomium und der Deuteronomiker*. Bielefeld and Leipzig: J. C. Hinrich, 1872.

Lagrange, M.-J. "Le Decret 'Lamentabili Sane Exitu' et la critique historique." *Revue biblique* NS4 (1904), pp. 543-554.

----------. "Inspiration des livres saints." *Revue biblique* 5 (1896), pp. 199-220.

----------. "L'Inspiration et les exigences de la critique." *Revue biblique* 5 (1896), pp. 496-518.

----------. "L'interpretation de la Sainte Ecriture par l'Eglise." *Revue biblique* 9 (1900), pp. 135-142.

----------. *La Methode historique*. Ed. augmentée. Paris: Victor Lecoffre, 1904.

----------. *M. Loisy et le modernisme: A propos des Memoires*. Juvisy: Editions du Cerf, 1932.

----------. *Le Sens du christianisme d'après l'exégèse allemande*. Paris: Victor Lecoffre, 1918.

LaSor, William Sanford. "The *Sensus Plenior* and Biblical Interpretation." In *Scripture, Tradition, and Interpretation: Essays Presented*

to Everett F. Harrison. Ed. W. Ward Gasque. Grand Rapids: William
B. Eerdmans Publishing Co., 1978, pp. 260- 277.

Loisy, Alfred. *Etudes bibliques.* Paris: Alphonse Picard, 1903.

----------. *The Gospel and the Church.* Trans. Christopher Home.
Lives of Jesus. Ed. Leander Keck. Philadelphia: Fortress Press, 1976.

----------. *My Duel with the Vatican.* Trans. Richard W. Boynton. New
York: E. P. Dutton, Inc., 1924.

----------. *Simples réflexions.* Paris: Nourry, 1908.

Lohfink, Norbert. "Die Abänderung der Theologie der priesterlichen Geschichtswerk im Segen des Heiligkeitsgesetzes: Zu Lev 26, 9.
11-13." In *Wort und Geschichte: Festschrift Karl Elliger.* Eds. Hartmut
Gese and Hans Peter Rüger. Alter Orient und Altes Testament, 18.
Kevelaer: Butzon and Bercker, 1973, pp. 107-113.

----------. "Das Alte Testament und die Krise des kirchlichen Amts."
Stimmen der Zeit 185 (1970), pp. 269-276.

----------. "Der Bundesschluss im Land Moab: Redaktions ges-
chichtliches zu Dt 28, 69-32, 47." *Biblische Zeitschrift* NF 6 (1962), pp.
32-56.

----------. "Die historische und die christliche Auslegung des Alten
Testaments." *Stimmen der Zeit* 178 (1966), pp. 98-112.

----------. "Katholische Bibelwissenschaft und historischkritische
Methode." *Stimmen der Zeit* 177 (1966) pp. 330-344.

----------. "Das Siegeslied am Schilfmeer." In *Das Siegeslied am
Schilfmeer: Christliche Auseinandersetzung mit dem Alten Testament.*
Frankfurt: Josef Knecht, 1965, pp. 102-128.

----------. "Über die Irrtumslosigkeit und die Einheit der Schrift."
Stimmen der Zeit 174 (1964), pp. 161-181.

McKenzie, John L. "Problems of Hermeneutics in Roman Catholic
Exegesis." *Journal of Biblical Literature* 77 (1958), pp. 197- 204.

Megivern, James J., ed. *Official Catholic Teachings: Bible Interpretation.* Wilmington, NC: McGrath, 1978.

Meyerhoff, Hans. *Time in Literature.* Berkeley: University of
California Press, 1955.

Murphy, Roland O. "The Relationship between the Testaments."
Catholic Biblical Quarterly 26 (1964), pp. 349-359.

Norden, Eduard. *Die antike Kunstprosa vom VI. Jahrhundert v. Chr
bis die Zeit der Renaissance.* Second edition, 2 vols. Leipzig: B. G. Teub-
ner, 1909.

Noth, Martin. "Die Vergegenwärtigung des Alten Testaments in der
Verkundigung." *Evangelische Theologie* 12 (1952/53), pp. 6-17.

Pederson, Johannes. *Israel: Its Life and Culture I-II*. London: Oxford University Press, 1940.

Rahner, Karl. *Inspiration in the Bible*. Trans. Charles H. Henkey. New York: Herder and Herder, 1961.

Robinson, James. "Scripture and Theological Method: A Protestant Study in *Sensus Plenior*." *Catholic Biblical Quarterly* 27 (1965), pp. 6-27.

Schroeder, Francis J. *Pére Lagrange and Biblical Inspiration*. Washington: Catholic University of America Press, 1954.

Steinmann, Jean. *Biblical Criticism*. Trans. J. R. Foster. Vol. 63, *The Twentieth Century Encyclopedia of Catholicism*. Ed. Henri Daniel-Rops. New York: Hawthorn Books, 1958.

Stephenson, Keith D. "Roman Catholic Biblical Interpretation: Its Ecclesiastical Context in the Past Hundred Years." *Encounter* 34 (1972), pp. 303-328.

Strawson, P. F. "On Referring." *Mind* 59 (1950), pp. 320-344.

Vawter, Bruce. "The Fuller Sense: Some Considerations." *Catholic Biblical Quarterly* 26 (1964), pp. 85-96.

Vidler, Alec R. *The Modernist Movement in the Roman Church: Its Origins and Outcome*. Cambridge: Cambridge University Press, 1934.

Weisengoff, John P. Rev. of *Problèmes et méthode d'exégèse théologique*, ed. Lucien Cerfaux. *Catholic Biblical Quarterly* 14 (1952), pp. 83-85.

Wellek, René and Austin Warren. *Theory of Literature*. Third edition. New York: Harcourt, Brace, and World, 1956.

Wimsatt, William K., Jr., and Aubrey Beardsley. *The Verbal Icon: Studies in the Meaning of Poetry*. Lexington, KY: Noonday Press, 1954.

Wittgenstein, Ludwig. *Philosophische Untersuchungen. Philosophical Investigations*. Ed. G. E. M. Anscombe. Third, bilingual, edition. New York: The Macmillan Co., 1970.

----------. *Über Gewissheit. On Certainty*. Eds. G. E. M. Anscombe and G. H. von Wright. Trans. Denis Paul and G. E. M. Anscombe. Bilingual edition. New York and Evanston: J. and J. Harper Editions, 1969.

Zimmerli, Walther. "Sinaibund und Abrahambund, Ein Beitrag zum Verständnis der Priesterschrift." *Theologische Zeitschrift* 16 (1960), pp. 268-280.